The Cinema of Wim Wenders
From Paris, France to *Paris, Texas*

Studies in Cinema, No. 41

Diane M. Kirkpatrick, Series Editor

Professor, History of Art
The University of Michigan

Other Titles in This Series

The Cinema of Wim Wenders
From Paris, France to *Paris, Texas*

by
Kathe Geist

U·M·I Research Press

Ann Arbor / London

Produced and distributed by
UMI Research Press
an imprint of
University Microfilms Inc.
Ann Arbor, Michigan 48106

Library of Congress Cataloging in Publication Data

Geist, Kathe, 1948-
　The cinema of Wim Wenders : from Paris, France to Paris, Texas /
by Kathe Geist.
　　p. cm.—(Studies in cinema ; no. 41)
　　Bibliography: p.
　　Includes index.
　　ISBN 0-8357-2035-7 (pbk.)
　　1. Wenders, Wim—Criticism and interpretation.　I. Title.
II. Series.
PN1998.3.W46G45　1988
791.43'0232'0924—dc19　　　　　　　　　　　　　　　　87-24076
　　　　　　　　　　　　　　　　　　　　　　　　　　　　CIP

British Library CIP data is available.

In memory of my father

Contents

Wim Wenders
(*Photograph by Edward Lachman; courtesy Gray City, Inc.*)

Preface

In 1984, Wim Wenders' *Paris, Texas,* a collaboration with American playwright Sam Shepard, won the coveted Golden Palm in Cannes, played in cities across the United States, was broadcast on cable television, and became available on video cassette for home viewing. For a filmmaker hitherto known only to a handful of scholars, critics, and erudite film buffs, the extent of this popular success was astonishing. The filmmaking odyssey that in many ways culminated in *Paris, Texas* began in 1966 in Paris, France, where Wenders studied printmaking, haunted Henri Langlois' Cinémathèque, and began his first 16mm short. A Düsseldorfer, Wenders returned to Germany in 1967 to attend film school in Munich and went on to become a leading figure in the movement known as the New German Cinema, an auteur cinema that gained worldwide recognition in the 1970s. Seeking to break with a dying industry and breathe new life and meaning into German film, many young filmmakers took part in the movement though only a handful are well-known outside Germany: Rainer Werner Fassbinder, who died in 1982, Werner Herzog, Volker Schlöndorff, Margarethe von Trotta, and Wim Wenders. Neither mystical like Herzog nor overtly political like Fassbinder, Schlöndorff and von Trotta, Wenders was characterized as the "anthropologist" of the New German Cinema,[1] for his films delineated the loneliness, isolation, and confusion that engulfed many young people of his generation. In *Paris, Texas,* the image of the lonely German blends into that of the Westerner, an icon of loneliness that had intrigued and haunted Wenders throughout his life as much as it had Sam Shepard.

Still an isolated triumph, *Paris, Texas* is less important to the chronicler of Wenders at mid-career than the body of German feature films the director made between 1971 and 1977; *The Goalie's Anxiety at the Penalty Kick (Die Angst des Tormanns beim Elfmeter,* 1971); *The Scarlet Letter (Der scharlachrote Buchstabe,* 1973); *Alice in the Cities (Alice in den Städten,* 1974); *Wrong Move (Falsche Bewegung,* 1975); *Kings of the Road (Im Lauf der Zeit,* 1976); and *The American Friend (Der amerikanische Freund,* 1977).[2] Standing as a unit, their significance becoming more sharply etched with the passing of time, they document a movement, a generation, and an artist coming of age.

In the early 1960s the New German Cinema arose phoenix-like from the ashes of an old German cinema which had produced little of merit since 1933. A disparate group of filmmakers with the common goal of revitalizing an industry that was all but dead, their efforts met with resistance from the old industry and indifference from the general public. However, with financial assistance from government agencies and German television, the new movement blossomed in the 1970s and gained international recognition so great that the German public itself began to take note of and pride in its new filmmakers. (When, in 1984, a dispute between Wenders and his German distributor caused *Paris, Texas* to be withheld from German theaters, bus tours from Munich to Zurich were organized so that Germans could see Wenders' latest success.)

In particular the new filmmakers became heroes for the young in Germany. The generation which had seen its hopes for social change crushed in the 1970s by the excesses of leftist terrorism and official reaction to that terrorism, saw in the new cinema proof that change was possible.

No director was more representative of the postwar generation than Wim Wenders, who documented the depressed state, the "desperation or cowardice of people who a couple of years before were still very enthusiastic."[3] All over the world in 1968 the children of the postwar era protested, ostensibly against the Vietnam War and the moral vacuity of international capitalism, but more, perhaps, against a certain spiritual emptiness that the highly commercialized postwar world had bequeathed them. As the children of a defeated nation, young Germans in particular felt nagged by a sense of vacuum. They had grown up unable to take pride in a country whose name was still linked with genocide. Mentored by the American Occupation, they rejected much of the supposedly "contaminated" culture of Germany and embraced the far-flung culture of America. When that foster culture's feet of clay were exposed in the Vietnam era, young Germans were doubly disenchanted. Their protests in 1968 were intense and often violent; when the protest movement degenerated into terrorism, the tragedy touched many personally.

Wenders' films are not political in the sense that they discuss political events. Rather they chronicle the depression, the emptiness, the longing for meaningful contact in society by individuals, usually men, who have dropped out of that society. When asked if Wenders' films portrayed the mainstream of German youth or only the outsiders, his film school colleague Bernd Schwamm replied, "The outsiders, of course. But there were so *many* of them then."[4] The "outsiders" began to show up statistically by 1975 when a survey of German youth (approximately ten years younger than Wenders' cohort) labeled 37 percent of the respondents "*Verdrossene,*" characterized as individualists and drop-outs who were skeptical, fatalistic, ambivalent, and resigned.[5] An audience was waiting for Wenders. When *Kings of the Road* was released in 1976, it broke house records in Munich and Berlin.[6]

More than those of the other internationally acclaimed new German directors, Wenders' films and career chronicle the ascent of the New German Cinema. He was in the first graduating class of Munich's Hochschule für Fernsehen und Film, one of two federally funded film schools created in 1967 in response to protests of national indifference to young talent. After film school, Wenders won a grant from the Kuratorium junger deutscher Film, a government agency granting subsidies for first features, to make *The Goalie's Anxiety*. He was one of the founders of Filmverlag der Autoren, a production and distribution cooperative originally owned by thirteen young directors. While in film school, Wenders worked as a critic and board member for *Filmkritik* and helped lead a new movement in German film criticism, which, echoing the *nouvelle vague,* lauded the formerly denigrated films of Hollywood, films the young critics had grown up on.

The new movement is also documented within Wenders' films, which make frequent reference to American film heroes like Ford, Hawks, Siegel, Fuller, and Ray as well as to New German films: *Wrong Move* includes a clip from Jean-Marie Straub and Daniele Huillet's *Chronicle of Anna Magdalena Bach* and the title frame of Peter Lilienthal's *La Victoria*. The Bach film appears as a television broadcast, indicating a major source of NGC financing. *Kings of the Road* discusses the cinema desert left by the German film establishment and the American distributors, and pays tribute to prewar and emigré director Fritz Lang.

In 1978 Wenders came to the United States on a contract to direct *Hammett* for Francis Ford Coppola. Work on *Hammett* lasted until 1982 during which time Wenders completed two highly introspective films in English, *Lightning over Water* (1980) and *The State of Things* (1982). In 1985 he returned to Germany to work in Berlin and in 1987 completed *The Sky over Berlin (Der Himmel über Berlin),* his first German-language film in a decade.

This book covers Wenders' first group of German films (1967-1977) as well as the films made between 1978 and 1985 while he resided in the United States. Released as this book goes to press, *The Sky over Berlin* will not be discussed here although credits for it appear in the Filmography (appendix A).

For help in researching and writing this book I wish to thank the following individuals and institutions: Wim Wenders, who took time out of a busy schedule at a difficult time for a lengthy interview; Claus Carlé, Tankred Dorst, Helmut Färber, Michael Hild, Lisa Kreuzer, Wolfgang Längsfeld, Martin Müller, Bernd Schwamm, and Jimmy Vogler, all of whom graciously consented to interviews; Bauer Film, Bayerischer Rundfunk, the Deutsche Kinemathek (Berlin), the Deutsches Jugendinstitut (Munich), Film Forum (New York), the Filmmuseum (Munich), Filmverlag der Autoren, Gray City, Inc., the Hochschule für Fernsehen und Film (Munich), Road Movies, and Westdeutscher Rundfunk for making films and other materials available to me; and the Fulbright Commission for financing eighteen months of research in Munich. Additional thanks to William Alexander, Ray Blanco, Hubert Cohen, Doris Herzog, Diane Kirkpatrick, Victor Miesel, Enno Patalas, John Pierson, Tom Prassis, Franz Riedl, Walter Seidler, and Chris and Lilyan Sievernich.

1

Prologue

On May 6, 1945, Germany surrendered unconditionally to the Allied Forces. On August 8–9, 1945, the first atomic bombs were dropped on Hiroshima and Nagasaki; on August 10, Japan too surrendered unconditionally. On August 14, 1945, Wilhelm Ernst Wenders was born in Düsseldorf, Germany, in the British Occupation Zone. His relatives lived in the American Zone.

> My first memories of America were of a mythical country where everything was much better. It was chocolate and chewing gum [gifts American soldiers often gave children]. One of my cousins had an uncle in the United States and thanks to him had a toy gun and an Indian headress that I loved. In Germany at that time there weren't any toys and the only ones I knew were American toys, which were really marvelous. . . . At 3 or 4 I didn't know my country was occupied. I had no idea. . . . Certainly I saw troops, soldiers, tanks, but for me it was all spectacle.[1]

At 11, Wenders started listening to the "Hit Parade" on the Armed Forces Radio Network (AFN). "Those tunes, those rhythms, and also the films made America into something very specific for me."[2]

Wenders' early fascination with things American was not an isolated nor an accidental phenomenon for the Occupation armies made a direct bid for the hearts and minds of Germans, particularly German children. As part of its Allied re-education program in Germany, American films were distributed by the Army and shown in local theaters. Each program consisted of feature films such as *The Human Comedy, It Started with Eve, The Maltese Falcon, Abe Lincoln in Illinois,* and *Young Tom Edison,* newsreels, and short OWI documentaries. In 1946 Robert Joseph, American Deputy Film Officer for Germany, reported the success of film programs with German children.

> The second success of the film operation was winning over the German children to American films. . . . Kids' matinees . . . were instituted early in the film operation in Berlin to test child reactions. . . .
>
> We suspected in the beginning that the elders would keep the children from our houses, but in the many theaters in which we instituted these Saturday and Sunday morning programs we had 100% attendance. I watched one group come out of a Saturday morning showing of a program which included *Autobiography of a Jeep* [an OWI documentary]. There happened to be some jeeps parked down the street. A flock of [the children] wandered down to the vehicles and inspected them much as the Indians might have looked at Cortez' or Pizzaro's horses. . . .[3]

The American films that adults as well as children embraced so enthusiastically were those made in Hollywood between 1937 and 1944, years when American films had been banned from Germany. The film programs were intended to teach democratic values and win over the Germans, but Hollywood producers soon recognized the advantage of dumping in Germany films which had already made their money at home. A program begun with laudable intentions became a stepping stone to exploitative practices which did much to cripple the German film industry after the war.

The Hitler years had also done irreparable damage to the German film industry. Hundreds of producers, writers, directors, actors, and technicians had been forced to flee, among them luminaries such as Elizabeth Bergner, Paul Czinner, William Dieterle, E. A. Dupont, Fritz Lang, Peter Lorre, Joe May, Max Ophuls, Erich Pommer, Otto Preminger, Emerich Pressburger, Max Reinhardt, Lotte Reiniger, Hans Richter, Eugen Schüfftan, Robert Siodmak, Douglas Sirk, Edgar Ulmer, Conrad Veidt, and Billy Wilder. Most of them did not return. Hollywood had already lured away German film talent before 1933: Marlene Dietrich, Karl Freund, Greta Garbo, Paul Leni, Ernst Lubitsch, and F. W. Murnau; but a fertile exchange between Hollywood and Berlin would doubtless have continued had Hitler's anti-Semitism, censorship, and war not intervened. After the war a conservative, self-conscious industry did nothing to welcome the emigrés back. Most who returned worked in the theater rather than in the film industry, many in Vienna. Lang, Lorre, Siodmak, and Sirk tried making films in the Federal Republic after the war with little success. "German critics at that time seemed to have a barely conscious resentment of the emigrés of the thirties like Lang and Dietrich. . . .[I]n 1959 [Lang] was wryly amused to find 'Yankee Go Home' chalked on the walls of both the studio and locations."[4] Thus the cream of a generation's talent was lost to Germany.

Under Joseph Goebbels' watchful eye, the talent that stayed behind was continuously demoralized. Only two filmmakers produced great films in the Nazi period—Leni Riefenstahl, who was not subjected to Goebbels' interference because of her close relationship to Hitler, and Helmut Käutner, whose constant struggle with the censors apparently produced a creative tension beneficial to his art.[5]

After the war German actors, directors, writers, and exhibitors were systematically "de-Nazified" and gradually returned to work. Those who had been Nazi Party members generally did not work again until the 1950s; others began working right away under the supervision of the occupying forces. Although their scripts were still censored by the Allies, filmmakers enjoyed vastly more freedom. The best known films of the immediate postwar period, the so-called *Trümmerfilme* (rubble films) because they were filmed among the ruins of Berlin, examined the plight of Germany in the aftermath of war, recalled Nazi atrocities, and sought their causes. They include Wolfgang Staudte's *The Murderers Are among Us* (*Die Mürder sin unter uns,* 1947) and *Rotation* (1949), Kurt Maetzig's *Marriage in Shadow* (*Ehe im Schatten,* 1948), Erich Engle's *The Blum Affair* (*Affaire Blum,*

1949), Robert Jugert's *Film without a Title* (*Film ohne Title*, 1947), Harald Braun's *Between Yesterday and Tomorrow* (*Zwischen Gestern und Morgen*, 1947), Robert Stemmle's *Ballad of Berlin* (*Berliner Ballade*, 1948), and Käutner's *In Former Days* (*In Jenen Tagen*, 1947). Benefitting from the same conditions that gave rise to Italian Neo-Realism, namely poverty, the *Trümmerfilme* had the same honesty and roughhewn grace. Their triumph was short-lived, however. In the Russian sector, where Staudte, Maetzig, and Engle worked, oppressive censorship was renewed. In Adenauer's West, Germans began to enjoy their first period of economic stability and prosperity since World War I and wanted no more reminders of their recent past. Enjoying the fruits of their "economic miracle," West Germans sought a low profile in the world. Will Tremper (*Die endlose Nacht*, 1963), one of the few independent German filmmakers of the fifties, described the attitude of producers in that period:

> I believe that all the German films of the old producers were made so that you don't see anything of Germany. They are shooting films in Munich and Hamburg, but they try to make sure that no typical sign of these places comes into the background. They even do something with the identification numbers on the cars. . . . Till now [1967] you have never heard that there is even a political party in Germany. . . . They are afraid to talk about it.[6]

The American Occupation also contributed to the decline of the German film industry by helping Hollywood dump its wartime films on Germany. In order to insure the continued success of their film exports to Germany, the Americans insisted that no import quota be imposed on American films, a stipulation that no other film-producing country has ever agreed to. The failure of the Federal Republic to protect its own product joined the failure of nerve on the part of the German industry to create a downward spiral in the quality of films produced.

With the exception of films by Staudte (who eventually left the Russian sector), Käutner, and Bernhard Wicki (*The Bridge* [*Die Brücke*], 1959), the West German industry produced little of merit in the 1950s. The most popular genre was the *Heimatfilm*, a reactionary form which even when set in the present recalled a supposedly wholesome, apolitical, preindustrial Germany.[7] *Heimat* films regularly outsold popular American films and contributed to a box office boom in the 1950s that lasted until the end of the decade, when television finally began to take its toll on box office receipts.

By 1961 the industry had reached its nadir: the Berlin Film Festival announced that no prize would be awarded for the best German film that year because none was worthy of honor. Young filmmakers like Alexander Kluge, Hans-Jürgen Pohland, Edgar Reitz, Peter Schamoni, Haro Senft, and Herbert Vesely were winning prizes abroad for their independently produced short films and began agitating for reform in the German industry. According to Edgar Reitz,

> They had tiny green stickers with the slogan "Papas Kino ist tot" [Papa's cinema is dead] printed up on sheets, like postage stamps, and we all stuck them on our letters . . . and also in cafes, on lavatory seats, etc. It was an incredible feeling. . . .[8]

In 1962, twenty-six young filmmakers met in Oberhausen, which has hosted an an-
nual short film festival since 1955, and signed the now-famous Oberhausen
Manifesto, which proclaimed their readiness to create a new film industry in West
Germany. However, the Manifesto marked the conception rather than the birth of
a new industry. The group was divisive, and several years passed before they began to gain the recognition and funding they sought. Kluge, trained in law, was instrumental in winning legislative action for the group and helped to set up the
Kuratorium junger deutscher Film in 1965, which provided grants averaging
DM 300,000 for first features by new filmmakers. Among the first films financed
by the Kuratorium were Peter Fleischmann's *Hunting Scenes from Lower Bavaria*
(*Jagdszenen aus Niederbayern,* 1968), Werner Herzog's *Signs of Life* (*Lebens-
zeichnen,* 1967), Kluge's *Yesterday Girl* (*Abschied von Gestern,* 1966) and Ula
Stöckl's *The Cat Has Nine Lives* (*Neun Leben hat die Katze,* 1968).

Under pressure from the established industry, however, a new bill was passed
in 1967 which supplanted the Kuratorium with a Film Subsidies Board. The Board
no longer financed first features, but required anyone receiving aid to have grossed
DM 500,000 on a previous film within two years of its release. The Board required
"quality" films to gross only DM 300,000, but even with this reduction, few of
the young filmmakers could qualify because distribution channels were controlled
by the established industry, German and American. Unwittingly the Film Subsidies Bill encouraged producers of schoolboy comedies and softcore pornography,
genres which could compete with television and offered a quick return on in-
vestments.

Ironically television companies saved the new directors by producing their
films for TV. State-owned and less wedded to a profit margin, German television
could take risks that commercial companies would not. In 1974 the Film–
Television Agreement allowed films made with financial backing from television
to run for two years in theaters before being broadcast. The majority of Wenders'
German films have been partially or completely financed by television.

The vagaries of the German film industry are the larger context against which
Wenders' career as a filmmaker unfolded. Privately it began when his father Hein-
rich Wenders, a physician, gave him a hand-cranked projector, some old silent
comedies, and eventually an 8mm movie camera. "The only thing I asked for for
Christmas or my birthday was a new little Disney film or a Laurel and Hardy."[9]
As a child Heinrich Wenders had himself owned a 9.5mm movie camera (forerun-
ner to the 8mm) and had been very attached to the silent comedies of Sennett and
Chaplin. No doubt he wished to recreate his own childhood pleasures for his son.
As a youngster Wenders often went to the movies, usually to American westerns
or gangster films, an enthusiasm his parents didn't share. Eventually the family settled in the Ruhr city of Oberhausen, and Wenders began attending the short film
festival a few years after its inception.

Unlike his friends, young Wenders spent his pocket money making 8mm films but never considered the possibility of a career in filmmaking. In fact he first considered the priesthood, but his enthusiasm for that vocation waned by the time he was 16. He later articulated what he then only dimly perceived to be the source of his difficulty with the Church: "as a way of thinking, it has a lot to do with capitalism and oppression."[10]

Completing his secondary education in Oberhausen in 1965, Wenders went to Freiburg to study medicine, following the family tradition: "for centuries my family have been doctors and pharmacists."[11] He stayed in Freiburg for a year but found the authoritarianism in both the university and the hospital where he had taken a job as an orderly too oppressive.

> To cope with the university for six or seven years . . . and then to have to cope with a hospital system that didn't have very much to do with what I thought medicine was all about. . . . I would have liked to become a doctor, but not in this way.[12]

Wenders immersed himself in the humanities, chiefly philosophy, while still at Freiburg and then transferred to Düsseldorf, where he studied for one semester. An amateur painter, he applied to the Ecole des Beaux Arts in Paris where he was required to pass a preliminary course in life drawing, which was not to his liking: "I'd never done that before in my life. I was always interested in land-scapes . . . but I never in my life had made a drawing of somebody standing on a little . . . I mean it was ridiculous."[13] An acquaintance suggested that he study with Paris-based printmaker Johnny Friedländer, and Wenders spent the next six months in Friedländer's studio. The lack of curriculm and Friedländer's predilection for abstract art appealed to Wenders, who enjoyed working there.

The studio was closed afternoons, and Wenders spent his free time at the Paris Cinémathèque, where he saw as many as four films a day. His stay in Paris coincided with the peak of the French *nouvelle vague:* Truffaut released *Farenheit 451* that year, Godard *Two or Three Things I Know about Her.* More than any of the other young German directors, Wenders' career paralleled those of the *nouvelle vague* directors. (The long sessions at the Cinémathèque, writing film criticism before directing, an enchantment with American genre films. . . .) But he acknowledged the influence only much later:

> The films of Godard, for example, up to *Made in USA* and *Two or Three Things I Know about Her*, I saw and admired but with reservations. It's only now [c. 1982] that I realize how much they really influenced me.[14]

Summer in the City (1970) would include a clip from Godard's *Alphaville.*

He applied to the Parisian film school IDHEC, but was unable to secure a place and subsequently applied for the first class in Munich's Hochschule für Fernsehen und Film (HFF), which had just been created by the Film Subsidies Bill of 1967. The disarray of the newly opened school suited Wenders, who found he could do pretty much as he liked.

There was no tradition or anything. . . . So we were more or less able to tell them what we wanted. And just not attend the courses. And make our own suggestions and our own courses because they had no way of dismissing us because we were the only students.[15]

Wolfgang Längsfeld, who oversaw Wenders' studies, recalls him as ambitious and prolific. Whereas in the normal course of studies each student completes a short film exercise with actors, one short film, and a feature-length diploma film, Wenders, using his own money, made three short films (*Schauplätze, Same Player Shoots Again,* and *Silver City*) before he made his HFF-produced short *Alabama.* "By the time he graduated from the school," recalls Längsfeld, "he had already made a reputation for himself."[16] Years later, when he was working on *Hammett,* a fictional account of Dashiell Hammett's transition from detective to novelist, Wenders was asked if *Hammett* were a continuation of *Wrong Move,* his 1975 film about a young man determined to become a writer, Wenders replied:

Yes. If anything, then it is the continuation of the story of [*Wrong Move's*] Wilhelm Meister. Who also wants to become a writer more than anything in the world and likewise charges full steam ahead like a maniac to do it. And that is my story too.[17]

Temperamentally suited to the lone abstract world of the painter, Wenders forced himself to accommodate the gregarious world of filmmaking—an adjustment his films would chronicle.

Besides making short films, Wenders wrote film and music criticism for the journal *Filmkritik* and the daily *Süddeutsche Zeitung.* The work taught him more than film school, he says, because it forced him to concentrate on a particular film for several days at a time.[18] At the time he came to *Filmkritik,* a new trend in West German film criticism was replacing an older approach based on Siegfried Krakauer's ideological analysis of films. The young critics voiced a new appreciation of the American film similar to that of the *Cahiers du cinéma* critics of the 1950s.

Wenders became a leading exponent of the new trend, championing Hollywood films, writing mainly about American films from the forties and fifties. To these he added articles on *nouvelle vague* films and sometimes covered new German films (although he criticized Fassbinder's *Katzelmacher* for being "humorless to the last detail").[19] He rarely wrote on the established German industry, which, he felt, made films characterized by "brutality" and "scorn" for the medium.[20]

The importance of primary experience, what one sees and hears, was the guiding principle of his film theory. Eschewing ideological analysis, he viewed description—because of its immediacy and truthfulness—as an essentially subversive act, whether it came from the critic or the filmmaker. In a review of *Easy Rider* he wrote:

> *Easy Rider* is not a political film just because it shows how Peter Fonda and Dennis Hopper deal
> cocaine at the beginning, how they get put into jail for NO reason, how they are SIMPLY
> shot. . . . It is political first because it is beautiful; because the land which the two monstrous
> motorcycles drive through is beautiful; because the music we hear is beautiful; because we watch
> Dennis Hopper not only acting but also making a film: between Los Angeles and New Orleans.[21]

Wenders was intrigued by the unselfconscious simplicity of Hollywood films. Of Anthony Mann's work (*Man of the West, The Far Country, Naked Spur*) he wrote: "The actors only leave the locations when everything that could happen there is over. And everything that happens is apparent. Not even the faces pose any riddles."[22] While Wenders wrote about Hollywood, a number of young filmmakers were making films in an American style: Rainer Werner Fassbinder (*Love Is Colder than Death/Liebe ist Kälter als der Tod*, 1969), Klaus Lemke (*48 Hours to Acapulco/48 stunden bis Acapulco*, 1967), and Rudolf Thome (*Detective/Detektive*, 1968). In commenting on these efforts in a review of Thome's *Red Sun* (*Rote Sonne*, 1969), Wenders pointed to the artlessness of American films as the characteristic he prized most.

> *Red Sun* is one of the very unusual European films that doesn't try to simply imitate the American cinema and thus prove it should actually have been shot in New York with Humphrey Bogart,
> but rather has taken oven a certain stance from the American film. . . . The STANCE . . . is
> evident in the consistent flatness of the shots, in the monotony of the optics, which contain only
> a handful of close-ups, in the banality of the camera movements . . . which are never more than
> is exactly necessary, in the incredibly washed-out colors. . . .[23]

Friends of Wenders at this time say his enthusiasm for America was boundless, though he also knew and wrote about the stranglehold American distributors held over German movie houses. He had worked for United Artists for three months in 1967 and wrote:

> During the time I was there, about a dozen movie houses closed. . . . I saw cinema owners trembling with anger or weeping or wringing their hands and entreating [because] they didn't get the
> films that would have filled their houses. Instead they had to book films and fulfill contracts that
> guaranteed them bankruptcy. Theirs were the small town and rural theaters. . . .[24]

But the inner struggle against what he would come to see as the "Moloch"[25] of American cultural imperialism, the struggle that would surface in most of his feature films and dominate *The American Friend,* had not yet begun.

2

Stories and Images: The Film School Period

Confronted during the making of *Hammett* (1978–82) by Hollywood's need for stories, Wenders pondered the role of storytelling in his earlier career. In his diary film *Reverse Angle* he stated:

> One would think that after ten feature films I would regard this as my profession: telling stories through images. But strangely enough I never quite believed that. Maybe because somehow the images always mattered more to me than the stories or, I should say, often the "story" was only a pretext for finding images.

The films with which Wenders began his career, the shorts and diploma film made while attending the Hochschule für Fernsehen und Film, were composed of images that only hinted at stories.

Wender's first short *Schauplätze* was begun in 1966. No viewable copy remains although two shots from the film were used to open his second short *Same Player Shoots Again* (1968) and are thus extant. In the first of these shots the camera moves back from a chair to a television set tuned to a western and then to a table covered with empty liquor bottles. In the following shot we see traces of a man running out of a telephone booth while the camera holds on the telephone receiver dangling over the ground. The rest of *Schauplätze,* whose title means "locations" as in film locations, similarly consisted of "after-action" sequences which began where a normal sequence would end: a moving playground swing, for example, which someone has just left. The film constantly represents a void.

The main body of *Same Player Shoots Again* consists of five three-minute loops in which we see only the legs and feet of a man (Hanns Zischler) wearing a long coat and holding a machine gun, running and stumbling as if he were wounded. After the first, each loop is tinted a different color: yellow, green, purple and blue. After the loops a shot of a Coca-Cola® logo is cut in, followed by a profile shot of the wounded man being driven away in an automobile. Two short pieces of music, reminiscent of music used in thrillers from the forties and taken from an old 78 record called *Mood Music* (in effect, canned background music for film and radio dramas), accompany the film.

The film hints at a gangster yarn. The two shots from *Schauplätze* suggests a den hastily left and an interrupted phone call; then we see an apparently wounded man running with his machine gun, then the same man being driven away either captured or rescued. According to Wenders, the film is a metaphor for a pinball game, the five loops corresponding to five balls and the title coming from the words that light up reading "Shoot Again."[1] The suspense is thus that of a pinball player, and what we see is less a gangster story than the evocation of a gangster *film,* which, joined with the references to pinball and the Coca-Cola logo, becomes part of an ensemble of American culture.

Wenders' third short, *Silver City* (1969), is a series of three-minute overhead shots of streets, taken in the very early morning from the upper floors of buildings where Wenders lived at the time. Two additional shots with actors hint inconclusively at a story. In one a man runs across train tracks; seconds later a train roars past. The early morning light gives most of the shots a soft blue tint against which the red, white, and sometimes yellow accents of car and street lights stand out. The last shot in the film is of a boulevard with cars driving over it in one direction only, producing a consistent flow of white headlights, this time against a black rather than blue background. The other side is almost empty until a group of cars streams in the opposite direction; the red tail lights create a sudden and exciting contrast to the white lights above like a school of exotic, luminous fish.

Each shot used a single three-minute roll of film, and the light-flashed ends of the roll were left in to punctuate each shot. Two frames of black leader were cut in at irregular intervals to imitate eyeblinking in accordance with a then-popular theory among HFF students.

Several years after making *Silver City,* Wenders re-cut the film from two badly damaged prints, added found material, and called the new film *Silver City Revisited,* the only version available today.[2] The film opens with documentary footage of a patriotic parade from the 1920s followed by three different shots of waves, all tinted blue and taken from documentary footage of the Irish Revolution, which Wenders had leftover from a compilation job commissioned by the Munich Stadttheater. Toward the end of the film a still color photograph of a Swissair prop plane is cut in and held for about three minutes. The garish blue of the sky and the airplane's red stripes create a jolting contrast to the somber blue street scenes. The still is followed by soundless footage of an old-fashioned television set tuned in to a Rolling Stone concert. (The film's only sound is romantic themes, again from *Mood Music.)*

Silver City Revisited is a poetic and contemplative study of flowing movement and soft color interrupted at various points by hectic movement (the Rolling Stones), harsh colors, and still photos. In his later work Wenders continued to play the jarring and the ugly against the lyrical, achieving in *The American Friend* a frightening synthesis of the two. With its inclusion of city streets, trains, an airplane, rock stars, and artifacts from the past, *Silver City Revisited* is a virtual catalogue of Wenders' fascinations, all of which would show up with predictable regularity in his feature films.[3]

The fourth short, *Alabama* (*2000 Light Years,* 1969), was produced by the HFF as part of its three-year curriculum. The title "Alabama" comes from a saxophone piece by John Coltrane while "2000 Light Years" is a Rolling Stones song and was the working title of the film. Both pieces occur in the film's opening sequence. For the first time Wenders told a story with a beginning, middle, and end, but was inconclusive with regard to detail. Again it was a gangster story. A precredit sequence shows a cassette recorder in close-up which plays "2000 Light Years," then cuts to a high-angle shot of a street lined with apartment buildings over which we hear Coltrane's "Alabama." Thus Wenders immediately establishes his twin preoccupations of streets and music. After the credits we see the street from the same high angle, then cut to a man entering his gang's hang-out. He is photographed close-up from behind against the light, which creates a silhouette image. He is the hero (Paul Lys), but we will never see his full face.

The black-on-white image turns into a white-on-black image of people in a room as the hero walks through the door. Young hipsters stand or sit at tables placed at either end of the room, some posed around a jukebox placed in the middle of the back wall. The hero paces back and forth in front of the others while the camera follows, keeping him in full shot. Point-of-view close-ups of the people in the room are cut in. One asks the hero, "You know what you have to do?" A man next to the jukebox throws him a gun. In the next sequence the hero is photographed from the back seat while he drives. He turns the cassette recorder on. The high shot of the street shown at the beginning recurs, and we see the man's car pull up and park. The hero enters the building; moments later he stumbles out. A cut back to the hero driving shows him with head slightly bowed, clutching his shoulder. The cassette recorder plays Bob Dylan's rendition of "All Along the Watchtower," an apocalyptic song in which a joker and a thief wait in a howling wind while unknown riders approach. "'There must be some way out of here,' said the joker to the thief./'There's too much confusion, I can't get no relief.'"

The hero reenters the now dark hang-out. His friends are motionless bodies on the floor. Keeping him in a high-angle full shot as he staggers to the jukebox, the camera dollies in on him. Grasping the side of the machine for support, he flips the selector, punches the buttons, and listens to the Jimi Hendrix version of "All Along the Watchtower." He stumbles to the wall, then turns and staggers toward the center of the room, his deliberate, stylized movements suggesting a ritualized death dance.

A third sequence photographed inside the moving car follows, but this time we do not see the hero. Instead the camera takes his position and photographs directly out of the front windshield. The light dims, a result of the aperture being closed down slowly, until the screen is black. At the point of total darkness the light returns, and the landscape continues to roll past the windshield until the light fades again into blackness. The anonymous hero is dead.

With their missing, inconclusive, or abstractly delineated stories, and their insistence on the void, the first four shorts form a unit. Such depiction of the void was fashionable at the time. One thinks of Michael Snow's *Wavelength* (1967), a

45-minute zoom shot during which characters come and go in a room and *perhaps* someone is murdered, although the audience, its gaze fixed by the camera, cannot be sure. Wenders admired *Wavelength,* had written about it,[4] and had evoked its end (a close-up of a photograph of waves) at the beginning of *Silver City Revisited* with its shots of waves. In addition, the long takes of the stark, nearly empty apartment at the end of his diploma film *Summer in the City* recall the loft in *Wavelength.*

More than mere aesthetic imitation, however, the void was an emotional reality for Wenders and his HFF friends, who were unable to relate well to people. One sees this in the would-be narrative *Alabama,* where the actors move with stylized gestures that make them seem more like objects than people, where no one speaks, where the hero remains anonymous, and the camera dies for him. "I felt closer to machines at the time," Wenders told Jan Dawson.[5] The sense of alienation and void is conveyed by the Stones' song: "It's so very lonely when you're 2000 light years from home," a condition that Wenders felt characterized his generation.[6]

If Wenders made up stories to go with images, he also made up images to go with music. "For . . . two films, I had the music first and then added the film," he said referring to *Alabama* and *3 American LPs* (*3 amerikanische LPs,* 1969) his fifth short.[7] In his film criticism he frequently perceived images as intended to accompany music or as evocative of music. "The story of [*Easy Rider*] is also that of the music which accompanies it. . . . [The] songs don't simply illustrate the images in the film, rather the images illustrate the songs."[8] At the time the process, today turned into blatant advertising for record albums via MTV, still had novelty and integrity.

Wenders' love of rock music began because it was "the only alternative to Beethoven . . . because I was very insecure about all culture that was offered to me, because I thought it was all fascism . . . and the only thing I was secure with from the beginning and felt had nothing to do with fascism was rock music."[9] Soon rock began to mold Wenders' sense of art. "It was with rock 'n roll that I started to think of fantasy, or creativity, as having something to do with joy. . . . "[10]

At first rock was pure form for Wenders rather than narrative because as a youngster he had not been able to understand the English words. It was "communication, but not on the level of meaning."[11] He described an LP by the Creedence Clearwater Revival as "like a bar of chocolate, like a smooth flight over the Alps by jet in clear weather."[12] His sense of form, image, and sensation in rock music made him aware of its compatibility with film. He compared one song to "blue clouds in a panorama of Monument Valley from a John Ford western."[13]

3 American LPs, conceived with Austrian playwright and novelist Peter Handke, is based on one song by Van Morrison, another by the Creedence Clearwater Revival, and an instrumental by Harvey Mandel. In a voice-over Wenders and Handke discuss the way in which American pop music illustrates America, particularly the landscapes. "Films about America should consist entirely of panoramas, like the music does already," Wenders says in the film. Appropriately the film is composed mainly of panoramic shots and driving sequences. Wenders and Handke drive past gas stations and construction sites, and finally pull into a drive-in theater: Munich as middle-America. The Harvey Mandel piece is illustrated by a slow driving sequence at sunset.

Wenders maintained that even in his feature films "the music was never an ambiance or an illustration, but the story of the film . . . as important as the story or the characters."[14] *Alabama,* he claims, "is really about the difference between the Dylan version of 'All Along the Watchtower' and the Jimi Hendrix version."[15] Dylan's slow, nasal version accompanies the driving sequence after the hero has been wounded but before he finds his dead friends, while Hendrix' painful and passionate screaming accompanies the hero's death dance amoung the bodies of his friends. Closely juxtaposed on the sound track, the two versions are appropriately illustrated: the steadiness of driving with the steadiness of the Dylan version and the scene of carnage in the hang-out with the emotional extremity of the Hendrix version.

Although he insists that the songs in his films are not intended as commentary, Wenders admitted that after seeing the completed *Goalie* he realized that the words of the songs did match the film's action,[16] which is true of the early shorts as well. While the hero of *Alabama* paces up and down in the hang-out looking at his friends for what will be the last time, Hendrix' "The Wind Cries Mary," a song about inevitable death, plays on the jukebox. The final sequence, in which the camera's aperture is slowly closed down, is accompanied by the Stones' "The Lantern": "If you are the first to go, you'll leave a sign to let me know—Carry the lantern high!" As the light fades, the taillights of the car ahead continue to shine until the aperture is completely closed, a visual analogue to the lantern.

Wenders' only experiment in political dialectic was *Polizeifilm* ("Film about the Police," 1970), the last of his short films. Rooted in the tradition of the Keystone Cops, the film spoofs the Munich police, who, after the violent Easter Demonstrations of 1968, defused student demonstrations with gentle, reasonable methods called "tactics of tolerance" in an attempt to isolate the Left from the sympathies of the general populace.[17]

Staged action between a demonstrator and two policemen wearing stockings over their heads alternates with documentary footage of police headquarters and of actual demonstrations, stills of magazine advertisements showing "the good life," and frames of Donald Duck comic strips. As the actor–policeman chases the demonstrator down the street, a still frame of Donald chasing his nephews with a stick is cut in. Shots within police headquarters are rapidly intercut with a still frame of Donald saluting.[18]

The skits illustrate the right and wrong way to handle demonstrators. In the first skit the police beat a demonstrator to the ground. A voice-over whispering advice to young policemen explains that demonstrators encourage this violence because it shows the Establishment to a disadvantage. A second skit shows the correct way to handle demonstrators. A demonstrator enters frame left carrying a picket sign. A policeman enters frame right and offers him a cigarette, which he accepts; the two fall into an animated conversation. Another policeman enters from the left, walks quietly past the demonstrator and steals the picket sign in passing. Unaware, the demonstrator continues talking to the first policeman. This, the voice-over tells us, will mean the "political death of the dangerous rabble-rousers."

Polizeifilm represents a high point in Wenders' career as a political activist. Prior to making the film he had lived in a politically active commune, and during the Easter Demonstrations he was arrested for allegedly hitting a policeman with a cardboard box. Wenders denied the charge but was convicted and, a few months before shooting *Polizeifilm,* was given a suspended sentence. He alluded to the experience in his account of *Easy Rider.*

> Like when one listens to a record with earphones and in taking the earphones off is shocked to realize that the record was playing over the loudspeaker all the time.
>   I stood in front of Columbia's building and noted that I actually look like the people in the film, that I like Jimi Hendrix' music, that I am not served in many restaurants, and that I too have sat in prison for NO REASON at all.
>   And sometime, I thought, they'll shoot, too.[19]

Eventually *Polizeifilm* was judged too subversive to be aired by Bayerische Rundfunk, the company that had produced it.

Temperamentally Wenders was not really inclined to political activism. Even as a communard, he did not fit very well with his fellows: "I was in film school, and I went to see westerns every night, and they were talking about imperialism and fighting this and fighting that. . . . I had a hard time with them."[20] He inclined rather toward the introverted, passive art of the New Sensibility, which centered around the HFF.

The *Neue Sensibilität* or New Sensibility concentrated on the artist's inner self and was given over to personal reflection and a fascination with phenomena simply as phenomena. Peter Handke exemplified the trend in literature while Wenders helped to define it in film. While Handke explored and questioned the elements of language, Wenders and his cohort sought to return filmmaking to its primal elements. Wenders summed up the trend when he said:

> Right at the beginning, that was filmmaking for me: one set up the camera anywhere and aimed at something in particular and then didn't do anything, just let the camera run. . . . And the films which have impressed me the most are also those from the very early filmmakers at the turn of the century, who just shot film and marvelled at what they had captured.[21]

The New Sensibility's influence can be seen in most of the HFF diploma films. Spearheading the movement along with Wenders were Gerhard Theuring and Matthias Weiss, whose diploma films *Leave Me Alone (Why Did You Leave America?)* and *Blue Velvet,* respectively, exemplify the style. Both films are titled after rock songs, accompanied by rock music, consist mainly of long, uncut shots and driving sequences, and eschew narrative. Less severe than Wenders' HFF productions, *Leave Me Alone* and *Blue Velvet* are in color and have a romantic, feminine beauty.

In general *sensibilisten* films were characterized by cars and things pertaining to cars like highways and gas stations, by landscapes and sunsets, by the use of real time and infrequent cutting. They were often accompanied by rock music and made reference to pinball machines, jukeboxes, and record players, icons of the Americanized youth culture of the time. Actors were generally treated as objects, as interesting to the camera as a pinball machine and less dynamic than the landscape flying by in a driving sequence.

While the New Sensibility took on the positive responsibility of redeeming a jaded cinema vision, it derived in part from pathological sources because its inwardness and narcissism grew from an inability on the part of its practitioners to relate to people. "We scorned ordinary, bourgeois people," Wenders' colleague Bernd Schwamm explained about their HFF cohort, "but our elitism just covered up the fact that we didn't understand and really couldn't deal with people." Recalling Wenders' attempt to direct the required exercise with actors at the HFF, Schwamm said, "He had no idea what to do with them or how to tell them what to do," adding that Wenders didn't observe people very carefully because he wasn't interested in them.[22]

The New Sensibility, by its own admission, was also involved in the drug culture. Gerhard Theuring wrote of *Silver City:*

> In *Silver City* there are no crowds of working people who, still tired, hurry off to work morning after morning. . . . The world becomes a playground: one would like to be in one of these cars oneself, turning left, turning right. . . . Precisely because this film excludes itself from the drivel of everyday, it points in the same direction as pop music and drugs. . . . And why shouldn't a critic take drugs?[23]

Because of his own heavy use of drugs at this time, Wenders "ended up in a hospital,"[24] after which he began psychoanalysis.

Wenders' diploma film, *Summer in the City (Dedicated to the Kinks)* (1970), exemplified all that was good and bad in *sensibilisten* style. Its vaguely delineated story involves a man (Hanns Zischler) just realeased from Munich's Stadelheim prison, who is sought by his old gang for information he insists he doesn't have. He visits a series of former acquaintances in Munich, but when the gang becomes more insistent, he leaves Munich for Berlin. There he stays with a former girlfriend (Libgart Schwartz), visits another, and ambles through the snowy streets of Berlin. The next day his photograph accidentally appears in a newspaper story about the snowstorm. Fearing the gang will find him again, he flies to Amsterdam, having failed to obtain a wished-for visa for the United States.

The film is about depression, and the characters move in sonambulistic trances, speaking little and communicating less. Hans in particular seems enveloped in a mental cocoon from which he can hardly recognize other human beings much less interact with them. Characters tell about films, or books, or experiences, but they never converse. Mediated by these frozen beings, the story leaves little impression, but the camera, "just running" in the *sensibilisten* style, captures the silence, the emotional void, in strikingly stark black-and-white images: Hans bending down to open a bottle in an automat, lit only by a Coke machine, his taxi ride through Berlin at night, a lighted cigarette giving us brief glimpses of his face, a profile of the abandoned Libgart standing at her window after Hans leaves.

The film is scored with numerous rock songs, seven by the Kinks and two, including the title song, by the Lovin' Spoonful. Again the songs are much more the content of the film than is the story. Wenders explains them as "the only emotional contact the man [Hans] achieves," and elaborates,

> All the songs deal with summer and heat and sun and whatever, and the film was shot in January, and it was freezing cold. . . . But the film definitely had to be shot in winter. The whole film was more of a longing for better times, or summer, or affections.[25]

These the music provided.

As in *Alabama*, the songs also provide a commentary on the action. Conscious that the gang is seeking him, Hans listens to the Kinks' "There's Too Much on My Mind," and on the way to the Munich airport after a narrow escape he hears the Kinks sing "I am Free." Together Hans and Libgart watch the Kinks sing the bittersweet, romantic "Days" on a television broadcast, and just before the gang discovers him in Berlin, Hans hears the Kinks' ominous "Rainy Day in June": "The demon stretched its wrinkled hand and snatched the butterfly. . . ."

The songs describe an emotional depth which Wenders could not otherwise express. While rock music remained an important source of inspiration for him and a distinguishing element in his films, he would never again make it the subject of his films or depend on it for emotional content as he did in *3 American LPs, Alabama,* and *Summer in the City.*

The memorable images in *Alabama* and *Summer in the City* are the work of the now-famous Dutch-born cinematographer Robbie Müller. Müller began his career as assistant to Dutch cameraman Gerald Vandenburg and graduated to head cameraman with Hans Geissendörfer's *Der Fall Lena Christ* (1968), a Bayerische Rundfunk production. He met Wenders at this time. Just beginning their careers, they entered into a fruitful collaboration that lasted through *The American Friend,* Wenders' last film before coming to the U.S., and was resumed with *Paris, Texas.* "I could imagine working with another cameraman," Wenders has said, "but I'd miss the feeling I have of extending my experience with Robbie, of learning together with him."[26]

The film school period was one of extraordinary freedom for Wenders; such freedom in which to learn was a requirement of his personality, and he made the most of it. Static and awkward as his early films are, he grasped his essential subject matter: the void in human relationships, the lure of popular culture as a means of filling that void, and the importance of music. In addition he found strong images, many of which he would use again and again throughout his career, to articulate his subject matter. He also began the two most important artistic collaborations of his career, those with writer Peter Handke and cameraman Robbie Müller—story-maker and image-maker, their vision strengthened his own.

3

First Feature:
The Goalie's Anxiety at the Penalty Kick

Wenders met Peter Handke in the summer of 1966 when both were living in Düsseldorf. Three years Wenders' senior, Handke was already making a name for himself with avant-garde theater pieces. Their shared interest in rock music, film, and American pop culture as well as their shared notions of narrative practice led to a lasting friendship. Often Wenders read Handke's manuscripts before others saw them: while Handke was writing *The Goalie's Anxiety at the Penalty Kick* (*Die Angst des Tormanns beim Elfmeter*) in 1969, Wenders joked about filming it. In 1971 the joke became serious. Wenders took a tightly written script based on the novella to two television companies, Österreicher Telefilm and Westdeutscher Rundfunk, and convinced them to finance most of the film. Additional money was put up by the Kuratorium and Filmverlag der Autoren, a filmmakers' co-operative formed in 1971 by Wenders and twelve other directors, among them Hark Bohm, Uwe Brandner, Hans Geissendörfer, Peter Lilienthal, Thomas Schamoni, and Veith von Furstenberg.[1]

In the tradition of the "missing narrative" popular among the *Sensibilisten*, *The Goalie's Anxiety* is a crime thriller that never materializes. At the beginning of the film, soccer goalie Joseph Bloch (Arthur Brauss) lets the ball roll past him into the net without trying to block it, thus revealing his basically passive disposition. Benched for arguing with the umpire, he wanders aimlessly through Vienna picking up women. After spending the night with Gloria (Erika Pluhar), cashier at the movie theater he frequents, he murders her on impulse. Careful to remove his fingerprints but unmindful of some American coins he has left on the table, Bloch leaves Vienna on a bus, which he takes to the end of the line, a Burgenland village on the Austro-Hungarian border. Bloch whiles away five days wandering about the village, flirting with the maid in his hotel, Anna (Libgart Schwartz), and with former girlfriend Hertha Gabler, who runs a restaurant at the border. The village is preoccupied with the disappearance of a mute schoolboy who is later found drowned. Each day in the newspaper Bloch reads about the search for the schoolboy and the unraveling of his own murder–mystery via the trail of American coins he has inadvertently left behind. When a composite drawing

The Goalie's Anxiety at the Penalty Kick (1971)
Bloch (Arthur Brauss) and Anna (Libgart Schwartz).
(*Courtesy Gray City, Inc.*)

of him appears in the paper, no one in the village notices. Still reading his paper, Bloch goes to a soccer match where he counsels a fan to try to take his eyes off the other players and concentrate on the goalie. On the field a penalty kick is attempted: the ball lands in the goalie's outstretched arms, signifying, perhaps, Bloch's eventual capture.

A "deconstructed" thriller, *The Goalie* gives Bloch no motive for the murder, then saps his motivation to escape. Passive in the extreme Bloch flees to a border he cannot cross and makes no attempt to evade capture once in the village. In fact there is little classical motivation for anything in the book/film from the inane observations made by the villagers to moments of would-be suspense such as Bloch finding the schoolboy's body floating in a stream. Shortly after this discovery, Bloch crosses paths with a policeman—an encounter underscored by threatening music. The policeman does not confront Bloch, however, nor does Bloch mention the child's body to him. Nor does the juxtaposition of Bloch's discovery and the passing policeman ever add up to anything. No line of action develops in the film; like the fan Bloch meets at the soccer game, the audience is required to watch the goalie instead of the ball.

Although both the film and the book reflect *sensibilisten* aesthetics, Wenders found that the precision of Handke's deconstructive prose required careful attention to detail. It was impossible to set up and "just let the camera run."[2] He said:

> Someone said to me, one could only make *Goalie* with a 16mm camera, without a script, and somehow recreate what Bloch experienced. To me it was immediately clear that that was a totally impossible method, that one could capture very fortuitous and perhaps very beautiful things. But then it would have nothing more to do with the book, which has nothing fortuitous in it; it's all very carefully and precisely done, and I thought to myself, one must create images that are set up in a very defined way.[3]

An example of Wenders' careful translation of Handke's words into images is the scene in which Bloch comes upon the village schoolhouse. Handke wrote:

> Of course the house in front of him had only one story, the shutters were fastened, the roof tiles were covered with moss (another one of those words!), the door was closed, PUBLIC SCHOOL was written above it, in the garden somebody was chopping wood, it had to be the school janitor, of course, and in front of the school naturally there was a hedge: yes, everything was in order, nothing was missing, not even the sponge underneath the blackboard in the dusky classroom and the chalk box next to it, not even the semicircles on the outside walls underneath the windows and the other marks that, in explanation, confirmed that these scratches were made by window hooks; in every respect it was as though everything you saw or heard confirmed to you that it was true to its word. . . .
> It was as if he were drawing wider and wider circles. He had forgotten the lightning rod next to the door, and now it seemed to him like a cue. He was supposed to start. He helped himself out by walking around the school back to the yard and talking with the janitor in the woodshed. Woodshed, janitor, yard: cues. He watched while the janitor put a log on the chopping block and lifted up the ax. He said a couple of words from the yard: the janitor stopped, answered, and as he hit the log, it fell to one side before he had struck it, and the ax hit the chopping block so that the pile of unchopped logs in the background collapsed.[4]

Wenders shows the scene as follows: A close-up of Bloch's head as he walks; a static shot of the interior of the schoolroom which reveals a blackboard with writing, a desk in front of it with a pot of flowers and a stuffed weasel, and a wastebasket beside it; a pointer leans against the blackboard; some rolled-up maps stand in the corner; a chart with the alphabet beneath it hangs on the right and next to it a washstand with a towel hanging beside it. In a long exterior shot of the length of the building, Bloch turns away from the window. He walks toward the camera, which pans to follow him as he turns the corner and continues walking along the building. He glances briefly in another window and continues to the end of the building where he finds the janitor in the act of splitting a log. One piece falls to his right onto the pile and the other to the left. Bloch picks up the latter and throws it over the chopping block onto the pile. The sequence is accompanied by a dissonant chord similar to an electronic buzz, which continues until Bloch sees the janitor.

In translating Handke's prose Wenders cuts down on the number of objects included in the description, but his long hold on the classroom full of objects impacts similarly to Handke's minute description. Wenders has the janitor chopping wood out-of-doors and avoids the small catastrophe at the woodpile; however, he keeps Handke's basic idea of the woodchopping being the center of attention for a few moments. The dissonant music approximates the sense of Bloch's mental disorientation that Handke's description implies.

Wenders thus captures the essence of Bloch's absorption in objects and its relationship to his mental instability, but he does not follow Handke into Bloch's linguistic preoccupations: "moss (another one of those words!)" or "in every respect it was as though everything you saw or heard confirmed to you that it was true to its word. . . ." Handke's Bloch mulls over words the way he mulls over objects, trying to discern the relationship between them, but Wenders omits the linguistic aspect, probably because it is difficult to render on film and foreign to his own interests.

Instead Wenders concentrates on objects whose heightened importance recalls German films from the Weimar period. Bloch's rapport with objects is illustrated by the pleasure he takes in watching the records drop down in the jukebox when the bus makes a rest stop and his cuddling up to his radio in the subsequent scene. In many scenes the use of objects becomes an index of Bloch's subtle but mounting schizophrenia. Each time we see a room from Bloch's point-of-view (POV) the camera passes from object to object. In Gloria's apartment three static shots from Bloch's POV show successively an open window with a curtain blowing, two plants, and a window with a cactus to one side. The three shots occur after Bloch wakens in the morning and are repeated when he regains consciousness after committing the murder. Both times they suggest a sense of claustrophobia. Coming out of Gloria's bathroom, he adjusts the picture on her wall. After the murder he carefully wipes off the objects on the breakfast table. Instead of Bloch's facial reactions, we see only his interaction with objects.

When Bloch is in Hertha's kitchen, the camera pans to the right from the refrigerator to the sink to a chair. Hertha interrupts Bloch's contemplation of the objects; she notices the way he fiddles with the things in her kitchen and scolds him for it, vaguely perceiving that Bloch has displaced his feelings toward her onto the objects.

In three scenes in which Bloch awakens nauseous or confused, Wenders conveys his increasing disorientation through the objects in the room. In the first Bloch stares from his bed across the room. A POV shot shows a table, two chairs, and a lamp. In the second Bloch awakens in a close-up. The camera pans the room beginning from Bloch's POV showing table, chairs, and lamp again, then moves past the window to a triple mirror in which we see Bloch moving toward the sink; the camera comes to rest on Bloch throwing up in the sink.

Thus subjective and objective collide, stressing Bloch's schizophrenic confusion. In the third awakening scene the camera is no longer subjective. It moves in on Bloch's umbrella in the sink, then toward Bloch himself on the bed. It continues toward his shirt hanging on the end of the bed, then toward the triple mirror. In the mirror we see his reflection as he sits on the bed lost in thought. Wenders' camera moving over objects conveys the essence of Handke's description:

> In his room at the inn he woke up just before dawn. All at once, everything around him was unbearable. . . . The mattress he was lying on had caved in, the wardrobes and bureaus stood far away against the walls, the ceiling overhead was unbearably high. . . . A fierce nausea gripped him. He immediately vomited into the sink. . . . It seemed as though a crowbar had pried him away from what he saw—or, rather, as though the things around him had all been pulled away from him.[5]

The subjective significance with which Bloch invests objects causes them to become threatening, distorted, arbitrary. He asks Gloria if there are ants in her tea kettle. He learns that a child was killed when pumpkins were thrown at him. Later when he passes piles of pumpkins, threatening music on the sound track conveys their new significance. When Bloch leans over a bridge and sees the body of the missing schoolboy, the body is not shown in close-up; in fact it is scarcely visible. The preceding shot, a close-up of an apple on a tree branch, suggests the apple has more importance than the body and indicates the distorted value Bloch places on the objects he perceives. When Bloch asks the tax assessor, who sees objects only in terms of their price, to evaluate a stone he has in his pocket, the assessor tells him it is a common stone of no value.

Bloch reveals further distortions of perception when he tells Hertha that he never experiences or registers the first of anything but only the second, a remark initiated by a shot of two jars of preserves in her cupboard. He was almost run over by a car, he says, because he didn't see the first one coming, only the second.

Such "disorder of association" is commonly considered a symptom of schizophrenia, from which Bloch apparently suffers. Nevertheless he appears in many ways to be the sanest person in the film. The extreme rationality of the tax collector, the mindless babbling of Gloria, and the general idiocy of the villagers, make Bloch, despite his distorted perceptions and his constant probing and questioning, a sympathetic figure. In fact, Handke and Wenders both identify with Bloch, for a certain kind of schizophrenia is inherent in the filmmaker's or writer's craft, particularly within the *sensibilisten* aesthetic. Siegfried Kracauer, whose theory of film as the redemption of physical reality Wenders embraces, writes that film reveals the familiar to us, things we know by heart but not with the eye. "Once integrated into our existence, they cease to be objects of perception, goals to be attained. In fact we would be immobilized if we focused on them."[6] This is precisely what Bloch does: stops and focuses on objects; and it immobilizes him.

At the end of the film Bloch describes the goalie's anxiety at the penalty kick, another kind of immobility caused by focusing on too many options.

> The goalkeeper is trying to figure out which corner the kicker will send the ball into. If he knows the kicker from earlier games, he knows which corner he usually goes for. But maybe the kicker is also counting on the goalie's figuring this out. So the goalie goes on figuring that just today the ball might go into the other corner. But what if the kicker follows the goalkeeper's thinking and plans to shoot into the usual corner after all?

From this we understand Bloch's inability to respond to the ball in the film's opening sequence. At one point in the film the border guard describes his difficulty guarding a suspect in terms similar to those Bloch uses to describe the goalie's dilemma—he tries vainly to figure out which way the suspect might run. For Handke and Wenders the artist may perceive more than his fellow man, but he does not necessarily perceive it to better ends. For them everyone is trapped by his own arbitrary perceptions and valuations and an inability to act meaningfully or, indeed, to act at all.

Concomitant to the inability of *Goalie*'s characters to act is their inability to communicate. In *Summer in the City* Wenders' characters didn't even try to communicate, and indeed the difficulty of communication is a key theme in his early films. In all his films he stresses communication media: telephones, newspapers, televisions, radios, record players, tape recorders, film, writing, and painting. With the exception of record players, however, these media are usually misused and result in noncommunication.

In *Goalie* Bloch tries to telephone three times. The first time he ignores a warning that the phone doesn't work and loses his money. The second time he phones from the village post office but is cut off; toward the end of the film he goes into a phone booth and finds that the telephone has been ripped out. Bloch reads newspapers but is told that no one else in the village does. Anna tells him that the innkeeper's deaf mother watches television all day and insists on keeping the sound turned up even though she can't hear it.

While the motif of the misused communications device recurs in all of Wenders' early films, *Goalie* in particular is devoted to the misuse of language. In the cleverly written Handke dialogue, characters talk without communicating, responding only to key words and phrases or to outside stimuli, never to the content of the previous speech. For example, after Anna intrudes on Bloch, thinking he has already left his room, they converse as follows:

BLOCH: That was a misunderstanding before. You could have come in.
ANNA: Yes, that was a misunderstanding. I must have seen the bus driver earlier from a distance as he went downstairs and got him mixed up with you because I had assumed you were at breakfast.
BLOCH: I didn't mean that.
ANNA: What did you say?
BLOCH: There's too much furniture in this room.
ANNA: Yes, you're right. And for that there's too little personnel. The mix-up before only happened because I was tired. I'm overtired.
BLOCH: No. I think the rooms are simply too full of wardrobes and dressers and chests; one can hardly turn around . . . even talking is difficult.
ANNA: What do you mean by that? (Bloch goes out.) I didn't mean to drive you out!

At Hertha's tavern a similarly obscure conversation takes place:

BLOCH: It smells strange outside.
HERTHA: Somebody died next door yesterday.
BLOCH: Does your waitress wear orthopedic shoes?
HERTHA (*looking out the window*): That must be the bicycle.
BLOCH: Which bicycle?
HERTHA: The mute schoolboy's.
BLOCH: If these shoes came in other colors, they could become the fashion. Did the man who fixes wells return?
HERTHA: He couldn't even call for help.
BLOCH: Who?
HERTHA: The boy.

Elsewhere in the village linguistic communication has also broken down. According to the school janitor, the majority of the school children cannot speak in complete sentences. He calls them "more or less speech-handicapped." The woman whose husband died tells Bloch that when she sent her child to get a priest, the child couldn't tell him what was wrong and thus the church bells were not rung. The mute schoolboy reflects what appears to be a general condition even among the "normal" village children. The village lies on Austria's border with Hungary and Yugoslavia. Communication between East and West has broken down so severely that the border is mined. This *great* communications breakdown—the border with the Soviet Bloc countries—returns in *Kings of the Road.*

Although there was one anti-American joke in *Summer* involving Hans' innocent misreading of an Amoco sign as "Amoc" (once he discovered the final "o," he assumed it was an Italian brand), only with *Goalie* did Wenders' disillusionment with America begin to fully take shape. Interestingly, disillusionment didn't dim his enthusiasm; instead the two moods constantly confronted one another.

> It is something you treasure and at the same time you see that it's something that has taken over like a Moloch: the American cultural debris and the imperialistic dictatorship of the American film distributors.[7]

Goalie's Bloch is caught up in the general enthusiasm for things American. In Vienna he goes to see Howard Hawks's *Red Line 7000.* He plays jukeboxes, listens to a transistor radio, and carries American money around even though his team's U.S. tour ended a year earlier. He tells a pick-up about the forward he knew who went to America and disappeared only to turn up living in a trailer in Tucson, Arizona. Wenders details the penetration of American culture into the tiny, provincial village: a Coca-Cola truck passes Bloch on the road to Hertha's tavern; Hertha's assistant picks up a carton of Wrigley's gum she has spilled; American music plays on Hertha's jukebox; the local movie theater, to which young men come hot-rodding up on their motorcycles, is playing Don Siegel's *Madigan.* The American tourists in Vienna who talk loudly and obnoxiously at breakfast pose a clichéd anti-Americanism, but the real thrust is the trail of American currency that allows the police to track Bloch. This plot twist is not in Handke's book and serves as Wenders' personal comment on the betrayal of Germany, particularly the film industry, by American capital.

In part the anti-Americanism in *Goalie* reflected Wenders' growing awareness that as a European he was unable to fall back totally on the American style of film-making he admired so much.

> I see *The Goalie* as a completely schizoid film. . . . Which was appropriate, really, because that's the situation of the main character, Bloch. It was my own situation, too. . . . I realized while I was shooting *The Goalie* that I wasn't an American director; that although I loved the American cinema's way of showing things, I wasn't able to recreate it, because I had a different grammar in my mind. That was the conflict, in every frame. . . .[8]

Wenders felt his own style had broken through in one scene, one which derived from his short films; in this sequence, driving sequences, holding on spaces after the action has passed, recording time for its own sake, and emphasizing objects are combined with rock music.

> It's the scene where Bloch is travelling on the bus from Vienna to the border. It doesn't have very much importance in the film, it's a five-minute sequence, perhaps less: . . . the train is accompanying the bus and it's getting dark—that's the scene where I felt, even while I was shooting it, that this was the way it was going to go on for me. . . . I realized that this was my story, and I happened to find the right way of showing something. I lost this feeling again afterwards.[9]

The scene is primarily a driving sequence; Bloch sits in the back seat of the bus and talks with a fellow passenger, shown in a frontal two-shot. A stationary exterior shot taken from the right side of the road shows the bus approaching and passing. After the bus has passed, the camera remains focused on a car dump across the street. A close-up of Bloch's crossword puzzle follows, then Bloch's POV of the interior of the bus from the back seat. A close-up of the lady sitting next to Bloch follows, then a close-up of Bloch. The bus is then photographed from behind as it crosses a railroad track; the camera remains stationary; we see a train approaching as the bus disappears. A high-angle shot of the highway against a reddening sky shows the bus driving into the frame and pulling into the parking lot of a roadside restaurant. Each cut indicates a successive stage in the progress of the late afternoon and evening light, thus recording the passage of time. Inside the restaurant Bloch starts the jukebox, which blares "Red River Rock" by Johnny and the Hurricanes. A close-up of the records falling follows, then a close-up of Bloch laughing at them. A high exterior shot shows the bus pulling out of the parking lot and holds on the sunset after the bus is gone. The bus drives directly past the camera in an exterior shot taken at wheel level. A glowing cigarette ash hits the ground as the bus passes. In the next shot a train moves toward the camera. When half the train has passed, the camera moves along with the train. A shot into the bus's rear-view mirror while the bus waits for the train at a crossing follows. Bloch sinks down in the back seat while his transistor radio plays the Tokens' "The Lion Sleeps Tonight." A long shot shows the train shooting through the countryside.

The driving sequence with the accompanying train, the varying angles of the bus, the shot in the rear-view mirror, the close-up of the wheels passing, and the accompanying rock music would become important motifs in *Kings of the Road*, where Wenders would expand this short sequence into a film that was totally "his story."

Wenders' maverick notions of narration were confirmed when he saw the films of Yasujiro Ozu on a trip to New York in 1973.

> The importance of Ozu for me—after *The Goalie*, I think—was to see that somebody whose cinema was also completely developed out of the American cinema, had managed nevertheless to change it into a completely personal vision. . . .[10]

Ozu's indirect way of telling a story, his shots of objects and empty spaces which appear unrelated to the plot, and his preoccupation with time, process, and the void must have seemed to Wenders like a foretelling of his own style.[11] His initial enthusiasm for Ozu was based primarily on Ozu's late films, the only ones apart from *I Was Born, But . . .* (1932) available to Wenders at that time. Yet Ozu's early films frequently resemble the youthful Wenders more than his highly disciplined late films. For example, Ozu's early films abound with references to the West, particularly to American films, in the form of posters, clips, and obvious imitations of Chaplin and Lloyd, much as Wenders makes frequent reference to films and other aspects of American pop culture. In his 1930 *Walk Cheerfully*, Ozu filmed a car running beside a railroad track and being passed by a train with shots alternating between car and train—not imitating a Griffith chase scene but simply capturing the rhythm and the mystery of the passing train. Without having seen the film, Wenders echoed Ozu's sequence in *Goalie* and later in *Kings*. Wenders calls Ozu his "only master,"[12] and although some direct influence is observable in *Alice in the Cities*, which Wenders was writing when he first saw Ozu's films—in particular the heightened use of gesture, a marked characteristic of Ozu's style—Ozu functioned for Wenders as the best teachers should: he encouraged his pupil's own vision. (Ironically no assistant director with any creative potential could work with Ozu while he was alive because he was tyrannical on the set. Yet that tyranny produced films so perfect that, for Wenders at least, they teach by themselves.)

For *Goalie* Wenders completed the team that, with a few exceptions, would stay with him on all of his German films: Martin Schäfer assisting Robbie Müller on camera, Martin Müller on sound, Peter Przygodda as editor, and Jürgen Knieper as composer. Rüdiger Vogler, Wenders' alter ego in *Alice in the Cities*, *Wrong Move*, and *Kings*, had a small part in *Goalie* as the proverbial village idiot. A stage actor since 1966, Vogler had interpreted a number of roles for Handke, including one in his 1970 television film *Die Chronik der laufenden Ereignisse* ("Chronicle of Current Events").

The male camaraderie celebrated in *Kings*, *American Friend*, and several of Wenders' American films was no doubt inspired by the closeness the team felt as it worked together on film after film. A female reporter visiting the set during the *American Friend* shoot wrote that the team reminded her of "a closed male society,"[13] which it undoubtedly had become.

Benefitting from the schizoid tension he felt making the film, *Goalie*, as Wenders' first commercial feature, was a success in every way. He had translated Handke's ideas to the screen with a crisp exactness that surpassed Handke's own efforts in the frequently obscure *Chronik* and had won considerable critical acclaim. He had managed well-known stars and a sizeable budget without compromising his own vision. And finally he had assembled the crew and discovered an actor who would help him create his best-loved works. *Goalie*'s success opened the way for his next film *The Scarlet Letter* (*Der scharlachrote Buchstabe*, 1973), based on Nathaniel Hawthorne's novel. *The Scarlet Letter* would not prove so successful.

4

Losing the Thread and Finding It Again:
The Scarlet Letter and *Alice in the Cities*

Wenders filmed Hawthorne's *Scarlet Letter* because the idea of portraying the first generation of Europeans in America intrigued him. But as a German–Spanish co-production, the film soon got away from him: "If . . . you have to shoot it in Spain and all the Puritans are Spanish Catholics, you somehow lose contact with your ini tial idea."[1] (The film was shot in three languages and dubbed into German.) "I felt," he said, "as though I were sitting on a wagon without the reins."[2]

Wenders had not reckoned with the strictures imposed by an historical drama. Spontaneity and invention had to be sharply curtailed or one ran the risk of anachronism. Still a film student at heart, he told one reporter petulantly, "During the location shooting in Spain, it bothered me simply because I couldn't film any streets. . . . That really limited me."[3] Later he admitted, "I hadn't realized how hard it would be to have to leave out everything, every kind of *trouvaille*."[4]

Nor was Wenders able to cast the film as he wished. The need for bankable names brought Senta Berger and Lou Castel the title roles. Berger made a superficial Hester and Castel a completely wooden Dimmesdale. Wenders had wanted Russian actress Yelina Samarina for Hester and Rüdiger Vogler for Dimmesdale. Instead Samarina became a young Mistress Hibbins, while Vogler won a small role as a sailor.

Tankred Dorst and Ursula Ehler wrote a script for the film entitled "Der Herr klagt über sein Volk in der Wildnis Amerika" ("The Lord complains about his people in the wilderness of America"). The script was a faithful adaptation of Hawthorne's plot. Dorst's plays often deal with utopian experiments and the social constraints which undermine them, such as that of the short-lived Bavarian Soviet in *Toller.* For him the young Puritan colony was such an experiment, undermined by its inability to control or allow for human passion. Dorst, too, was disenchanted with the large production, its artificiality, and the miscasting. In addition he disagreed with script changes Wenders wanted to make and eventually took his name off the script.

Rewriting the script, Wenders and his assistant Bernardo Fernandez turned the plot into a semi-western. Social constraints were not inevitable in Wenders' youth-

Wim Wenders Directing Senta Berger in *The Scarlet Letter* (1973)

ful view, and his script attacked them broadside. Hawthorne's intricate analysis of guilt, penance, and the human soul became a tale of two lovers unfairly persecuted and repressed by a rigid and corrupt society.

To this end Wenders changed the character of Mistress Hibbins, Governor Bellingham's crazed sister, from a sinister old woman who dabbles in witchcraft to a young one who is simply neurotic. The young Hibbins serves as an alter ego for Hester and a vehicle for demonstrating the repression of women in Puritan society. She sees the sexual repression enjoined on Hester as the root of her own madness. When Hester stands on the scaffold, Hibbins entreats her to escape with her into the wilderness. Later she goes to the same scaffold and sets her dress on fire, while in another scene she comes to church wearing a yellow "A." When Dimmesdale reveals the letter etched into his flesh, she bursts into hysterical, vengeful laughter.

In Wenders' film God and Fate do not intervene to save Hester and her lover from what Hawthorne viewed as spiritual doom. Instead Dimmesdale's pride and ambition send him back to the congregation to give his Election Sermon. Instead of dying in Hester's arms after his confession, he is strangled by the new governor. Meanwhile Hester wastes no time wishing to be united with Dimmesdale in heaven but hurries with Pearl to the waiting ship only one step ahead of the governor's men, who, contrary to history, apparently feel that dissidents shouldn't leave the colony. No one cries over Dimmesdale, who is not simply spineless but shallow. "My father is dead; I'm looking forward to tomorrow," sings Pearl as they row out to the waiting ship. Hester's escape is made particularly thrilling when Pearl has to stop to remove a stone from her shoe; Wenders cuts between Hester urging Pearl on and the men pursuing her to create a last-minute escape worthy of Griffith, but foreign to Hawthorne.

Chillingworth, a robust backwoodsman seen sharing a campfire with his Indian guide, contrasts markedly to Hawthorne's old man crippled in body and soul. At the end of the film Chillingworth disappears back into the wilderness like *The Searchers'* Ethan Edwards, not, one supposes, to die from the loss of his vampiristic passion, as in the novel, but to continue living among the Indians as before.

The set in Spain, designed for shooting westerns, was remodelled, but never quite lost its 1850s flavor. Even the garden versus wilderness myth so frequently summoned by John Ford is invoked when Dimmesdale preaches, "If we break God's covenant, the blooming garden of America will become wilderness again."

German critics did not like the film. The kindest suggested that Wenders was simply the wrong man for this sort of job while another called him infantile and immature.[5] The most insightful complained that Wenders had abandoned the puritanism of his own style. The only favorable review praised *Scarlet Letter* at the expense of *Goalie*, hardly gratifying since *Goalie* was a fully realized expression of Wenders' art and thought while *Scarlet Letter* reflected Wenders' enthusiasm for westerns, children, and freedom from repression but little else. "Those who wanted a big drama weren't at all satisfied," noted Wenders, "those who wanted an historical film weren't satisfied, those who came for the stars . . . weren't satisfied either."[6] Wenders inserted a clip from the film in his TV drama "Die Insel" and parodied his critics' confusion when he had the family argue about whether they had seen a *Heimatfilm* or a pirate film.

The film's feminism, which reflects Hawthorne in spirit if not in detail, is anomalous for Wenders, who as of 1979 maintained that ". . . it's important that women make films about themselves and men make films about themselves . . . ,"[7] a policy he held to closely after and perhaps because of *Scarlet Letter*. "As a man you can't just make unqualified statements about women," he insisted.[8] The failure of the film and his disenchantment with Senta Berger caused him to dwell on his failure to develop Hester properly—("It's the only lead character in any of my films for whom I did not . . . have any feelings."[9])—and overlook his success with Yelina Samarina as Hibbins. Undoubtedly his interest in her as an actress and as a character was partly responsible for the film's strong feminist statement.

Also responsible was Wenders' genuine respect for women.

> With women I always had the feeling that they had all gone a step farther in this self-discovery. . . . The wives and girlfriends of men who didn't manage to live well with them were always well on their way to developing a feeling for and an understanding of themselves. . . . Only: the men weren't anywhere near this far along. . . . I think that the role of the oppressed makes one more able to maintain one's identity or to recover it than that of the oppressor. . . .[10]

His statement echoes one theme in *The Scarlet Letter:* the openly castigated Hester becomes strong, whole, and free while the socially powerful Dimmesdale is destroyed by his duplicity.

In *Scarlet Letter* Wenders, who claims that as a film student he was afraid to cut, is clearly the master of a classical narrative style. While Dimmesdale struggles to confess his adultery, Wenders builds tension by intercutting the congregation rumbling in confusion and Hester hurrying to the ship. In an unsubtle objective correlative, woodchoppers work while Dimmesdale and Chillingworth walk through the forest to symbolize the effect the doctor is having on his patient. At other times Wenders' style is less classical. Long holds on people, especially on faces, prompted Michael Covino to write about the "strange silences between people."[11] When Governor Bellingham trips and falls in the mud and later when Dimmesdale collapses after leaving Bellingham's bedside, Wenders photographs both in extreme long shot instead of bringing his camera in closer to create greater narrative clarity and dramatic tension. Possibly the model for these extreme long shots is that of Charlotte falling in Godard's *A Married Woman* (*Une femme mariée*, 1964). In any case they echo the extreme long shot of the dead child's body in *Goalie* and belong to the nonclassical style Wenders uses in his other films.

At times Wenders was able to fuse his own stylistic predilections with those of classical cinema. His love of panoramas is evident in several memorable shots:

Hester standing on a bluff while the beadle climbs up to get her, Pearl running along the beach to Hester, and Chillingworth and his Indian guide making their way down the hills into the settlement. The fusion is predictable since the panoramic shot is part of the vocabulary of westerns, precisely the point at which Wenders' style intersects with the classical.

A number of scenes recall the New Sensibility. Wenders cuts from the setting sun to Pearl in her bed and back to the sunset now grown darker, a sequence reminiscent of the sunset sequence in *Goalie*. Also reminiscent of *Goalie* is Wenders' dolly-in on Dimmesdale asleep, emphasizing, as in the previous film, the sleeper's vulnerability and isolation. (Wenders would use this set-up in several other films; when he did it in *Wrong Move*, Robbie Müller remarked, "Well, here we are again doing our travelling onto somebody who's asleep." When Wenders asked what he was talking about, Müller explained, "We do it every time.")[12]

A mixture of styles, the film was an exercise in eclecticism, at best an interesting failure, and Wenders was eager to leave well-financed co-productions to directors who had more forceful personalities or less demanding visions. "I want to work small again, preferably with direct sound . . . with a small team, nothing historical, nothing dramatic," he told a reporter at the conclusion of shooting *Scarlet Letter*.[13] These were precisely the conditions of his next film, *Alice in the Cities* (*Alice in den Städten*, 1974), in which he used his biggest dividend from *Scarlet Letter*, Yella Rottländer, who played a charmingly bumptious Pearl.

Alice begins with thirty-year-old Philip Winter (Rüdiger Vogler), a German journalist, returning to New York from a trip across the United States, on which he has been commissioned to write an article. But as he tells his publisher, "When you travel across America, something happens because of all that you see." Overwhelmed by the trip, Philip suffers from writer's block and joins the ranks of Wenders' paralyzed heroes. He is able only to take pictures and does so assiduously with a Polaroid camera, frequently developing and shuffling through them on camera as if trying to probe their secrets.

While attempting to book a flight back to Europe, Philip encounters Lisa (Lisa Kreuzer) and Alice (Yella Rottländer), her nine-year-old daughter. Lisa, who has come to America with her current boyfriend, hates the U.S. and is trying to get back to Germany. Her boyfriend, she tells Philip, is determined to stay but distraught at the thought of losing her. She asks Philip to take Alice to Europe a day ahead of her so that she will have time to calm her boyfriend while establishing an imperative reason for returning to Europe.

Philip flies with Alice to Amsterdam, a destination necessitated by a pilot's strike in Germany, but panics when Lisa doesn't show up at the appointed time. Envisioning himself saddled indefinitely with the nine-year-old, he plans to leave her with the proper authorities, but eventually yields to her protests and agrees to take her to her grandmother in Wuppertal. Unfortunately Alice has neither a name nor an address for her grandmother, and she and Philip drive endlessly up and down the streets of Wuppertal to no avail. Philip turns her over to the police but continues to linger in Wuppertal; in the meantime Alice escapes from the police and rejoins him that evening. Laughing helplessly Philip agrees to continue the search. As Alice astutely pointed out before he turned her in, he hasn't anything better to do anyway. Moreover the visit to the authorities has yielded some important clues: grandmother's surname and the hypothesis that she lives in the Ruhr district. In addition Alice finds that she has a picture of the house. To Philip's amazement, they find the house, but grandmother has moved.

They abandon the search and go swimming. A handsome woman (Didi Petrikat) takes them home for the night, but Alice rouses Philip early and insists on leaving. Out of money he heads for his parents' home on the lower Rhine. On the Rhine ferry a detective (Hans Hirschmüller) from Wuppertal spots them, for the police have been looking for Alice since she ran away: her mother and grandmother have been located in Munich. When the detective asks Philip why he never informed them that Alice had returned to him, he laughs helplessly: how can he explain that the absurdity of the situation precluded sensible action? The police put Alice on a train for Munich; when Philip can't pay his own fare back, she produces a one hundred dollar bill, hoarded for an emergency. Together they ride through the Rhine Valley to Munich: in the final shot they lean out the window together. Photographing them from aboard a helicopter, the camera flies higher and higher as the train disappears into the valley.

On the train Alice asks Philip what he will do when he gets back to Munich. "Write the end of this story," he replies. Despite the title, *Alice* is far more Philip's story than Alice's. He is the solipsistic, alienated Wenders hero, unable to communicate. As the goalie was obsessed by objects, Philip is addicted to taking Polaroids. In New York he tells former girlfriend Angela that the trip through America made him lose touch with the world. She counters:

> You did that a long time ago. . . . That's why you always need proof, proof that you exist. . . . That's why you always take pictures. . . . They're proof that *you* saw something. That's why you came here—so that somebody would listen to you, to the stories you're really just telling yourself.

Insistently dependent, Alice brings Philip out of himself, thus acting as a catalyst to his development. As a human relationship becomes his focus, he stops taking pictures and is able to write again.

Alice also influences Philip's relationships with adult women. The women he encounters in New York are unresponsive to him. Angela is tired of his egocentricity, and Lisa is too preoccupied with her own problems to notice his. But the woman on the beach, charmed by his nurturing of Alice, is willing to nurture him. While Alice's jealousy nips this last relationship in the bud, one imagines that Philip's future encounter with Lisa may end well. Before he meets Alice, Philip takes pictures of objects and landscapes. When on the Rhine ferry Philip attempts one last picture, his subject is a mother and child.

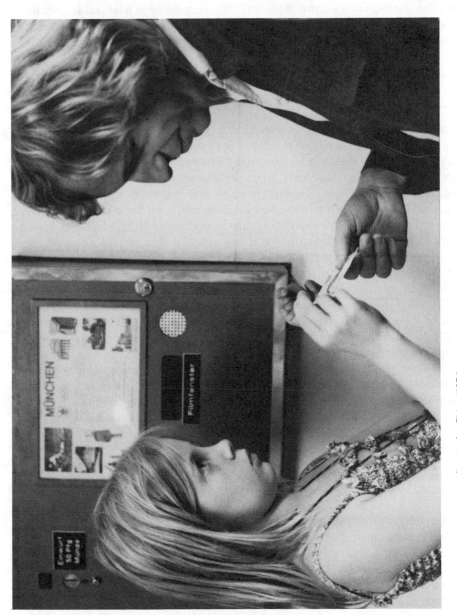

Alice in the Cities (1974)
Alice (Yella Rottländer) bails Philip (Rüdiger Vogler) out with a S100 bill.
(*Courtesy Road Movies*)

When Philip tells Angela that he has lost touch with the world, his words literally mean, "I lost my ability to hear and see." She tells him that one loses this ability when one loses one's sense of identity. With the ability to hear and see equal to identity, Philip's near obsession with a means for hearing and seeing—the Polaroids, for example—is understandable. About the Polaroids he confesses:

> While I was waiting for them to develop, I'd feel strangely uneasy. . . . I could hardly wait to compare the finished picture with reality. But even that didn't quiet me because the still picture caught up with reality and overtook it.

Wenders uses photographs to play with the idea of identity. Polaroids have no negative, and thus each has a unique identity. The photographs disturb Philip because they have a slightly different identity from "reality." The picture of the grandmother's house alters its identity when the characters learn that grandmother doesn't live there anymore. The picture hasn't changed, but its significance has. Alice and Philip have their picture taken in a photomat. Each frame is different and preserves the feeling of that moment. Feeling insecure about Philip's loyalty to her, Alice looks at the photomat strip to reassure herself of their identity as a pair.

Hans in *Summer* and Bloch in *Goalie* also have their pictures taken in a photomat as though seeing themselves in the instant photos might give them a clue to their identities. Alice voices this supposition when, after Philip insists he can't tell her anything about himself, she takes a Polaroid of him saying, "I want to take a picture of you. That way you'll at least know what you look like." But when she holds the finished photograph for Philip to look at, her own reflection covers the image, suggesting that she is the key to Philip's identity.

If Philip photographs obsessively, he reacts with equal intensity whenever he feels that hearing and seeing are being subverted or abused. He kicks his car radio when the DJ breaks in on a song before it has completely finished and destroys the television set in his motel room when it begins spewing commercials. Later he writes an essay about American television concluding,

> What is so inhuman about this television is not that everything is broken up with commercials—although that is bad enough—but that all of the programs become advertisements for the status quo. . . . No image lets you alone. They all want something.

(Later Alice tells Philip a nightmare she had about watching television: she had tied herself to a chair in front of a TV set when a horror film came on; she couldn't untie herself or even close her eyes and had to watch it.)

The "inhuman television" is only part of what made Philip's journey through America so intolerable. He tells Angela, "That was a horrible trip. From the minute you leave New York, nothing changes anymore. . . . I could only imagine that it would continue like this forever." Philip is an Americanized German who doesn't quite know where he belongs.

Alice in the Cities (1974)
Alice takes Philip's picture so he'll know what he looks like.
(*Courtesy Gray City, Inc.*)

Realizing that he won't find himself in America, Philip returns to Germany and, by chance, to the area in which he grew up. Back at his beginning he is able to seek and find that sense of identity which eluded him in the past when, confusing Americanization with America, he looked to the U.S. for self-validation. Drinking his Coke at a Chuck Berry concert in Wuppertal, Philip is home at last, able to accept the contradictions in his background. The picture of integration Wenders presents when he shows Philip at the Chuck Berry concert is important as a prelude to Philip's acceptance of Alice back into his life that evening, for Philip's self-acceptance makes it possible for him to accept Alice.

Although Wenders has said he chose the name "Winter" for both Philip and the Rüdiger Vogler character in *Kings* because it expresses the coldness and desolation these men suffer from, the name is strikingly similar to his own, particularly since "t" and "d" are practically the same sound in German. In any case, Philip's reaction to the U.S. exactly parallels Wenders' reaction to a three-week, cross-country trip he made during his second visit to the U.S. "America became a nightmare only ten minutes after I left New York. Such a huge country where every village and town was exactly like every other."[14] That monotony would produce such an extreme reaction was the result of the mythical expectations Wenders had of America.

> For me as a child America was never a place you could get to. It was totally mythical. Coming to America for the first time . . . was very disillusioning. Once I was there this paradise of my childhood seemed empty and rotten.[15]

In *Alice* the mythology of America is alluded to when we see a brief clip of John Ford's *Young Mr. Lincoln* on the television in Philip's motel room. At the end of the film Philip reads a newspaper with the headline *"Verlorene Welt"* ("Lost World")—John Ford's obituary. Not merely a tribute to Ford, the headline suggests the world that Philip/Wenders hoped to find in America and didn't.

Philip/Wenders' discomfiture with America has a long tradition in Germany, and their experience echoes that of countless German visitors to the United States before them. Historian Harold Jantz writes,

> The myth of America cultivated in Europe is a psychological reality far more important than the so-called truth about America. . . . When, as was to be expected, America could not live up to the high hopes Europeans cherished for her . . . the reaction set in, and America was bitterly blamed for not fulfilling the European dream picture of it.[16]

Even the details of their disappointment are the same. "Smaller cities often repelled the visitors [of the 1920s] with their monotony, their disarray, their sense of incompleteness, and neglect," writes Earl R. Beck, whereas in New York City "the noise, the bustle, the impersonality, the evidence of crass materialism . . . repelled [the German visitor]."[17] (Although Wenders and alter-ego Philip like New York

City, the other adults in *Alice,* including, uncharacteristically, a New York taxi driver, speak of it disparagingly.)

Yet Wenders cleverly resists the temptation to blame America for Philip's troubles and separates himself from his hero in this respect, for what he *shows* contrasts markedly with what the characters *say* about America. Wenders shows precisely those structures in America that fascinate him wherever he films: gas stations, old houses, trains; and he deliberately compares America and Germany, selecting shots of similar locations from both countries: rows of old houses, hot dog stands, elevated or suspended railways (in Queens and in Wuppertal), and virtually the same shot of Philip driving into a modern gas station in each country. Manhattan's skyscrapers become water towers along the Ruhr. If some of what Wenders shows of America seems dilapidated and junky, so does Wuppertal, where the street outside Philip's hotel is being torn up, and the Ruhr, where quaint, old workers' houses are being torn down. Industrial America and industrial Germany are not particularly different; Philip simply belongs in one more than the other.[18]

Alice's is the most beautiful view of America: from the top of the Empire State Building she pans the city through pay-binoculars, focuses on the most beautiful buildings, and at last follows the flight of a seagull. Children, according to Wenders, represent "a sort of ideal view,"[19] and in Alice he illustrates this view literally. At home anywhere, Alice's uninhibited truthfulness, spontaneity, and fresh vision are precisely the qualities Wenders' adults need to restore their damaged sense of identity. If *Alice* seems more hopeful than Wenders' other films, it is because Philip has direct access to these qualities through Alice whereas elsewhere his heroes must grope towards these qualities with only the aid of other adults.

The "ideal view" of childhood has, according to Wenders, "a lot to do with the films because the films try to have this attitude. . . ."[20] When Philip shuffles through his snapshots one sees that he has photographed the trademarks of Wenders' films: a plane wing, tall buildings, a car, the highway. Philip's need to establish his identity by taking pictures parallels Wenders' search through filmmaking. Since Wenders equates the child's view with filmmaking, Philip's discovery of himself through Alice extends the parallel.

The "ideal view" sees and hears as if for the first time. The little boy who appears briefly at the end of *Kings of the Road* has this view—he's writing down everything he sees. This is the principle on which Wenders prefers to construct his films: to include whatever he discovers of interest in a given day of shooting. For example, in *Alice* the organ at Shea Stadium plays while Philip sells his car at a used car lot in Queens. Subsequently there is a shot of the organ player. One imagines that Wenders' own process of discovery was much like that which he recreates for the viewer: he heard the organ, sought the source, and recorded both in his film despite their irrelevance to his story. In a second example, Philip sings lines from

Alice in the Cities (1974)
Philip under the boardwalk.
(*Courtesy Gray City, Inc.*)

the Rolling Stones' "Under the Boardwalk" at the beginning of *Alice* while he sits under an actual boardwalk. Wenders specifically sought out the location because he learned the song in Germany and had always wondered what a boardwalk was. The impossibility of working this spontaneously on *Scarlet Letter* made the shoot unbearable for him.

Thus Wenders' films became documentaries of sorts, and Wenders takes pride in this. For him fiction films are often the best documentaries of a time.

> The best documentaries of the 50s are surely the films of Howard Hawks and Nicolas Ray. That's because they weren't made to demonstrate anything. They were simply allowed to keep things as they were, and document the time when they were made.[21]

He sees his own work falling into this tradition.

> I perceive work as more documentary than manipulative. I want my films to deal with the period of time in which they were made, with the cities, the landscapes, the subjects, the people who work on them.[22]

He calls *Summer in the City* "a documentary about the end of the Sixties: about the ideas people had in 1969 and 1970, the way people felt."[23] *Scarlett Letter* "documented constraints under which I never want to work again."[24]

Conscious of working as a documentarist, Wenders shot *Alice* chronologically in South Carolina, New York, Amsterdam, Wuppertal, and the Ruhr. He shot a great deal more footage of Philip's trip through America than he actually used because in editing the film he felt he must get to Alice more quickly than a more extensive coverage of Philip's trip would have allowed. He faced a similar situation later with *Kings of the Road*, for which he shot much more documentary footage than the demands of his story would allow him to include. Later, in America, he would shoot several "diary" films in which he allowed his thoughts and images to wander unconstrained by a story.

Rock music again plays an important role in *Alice* as in his previous films, and this time Wenders, who calls jukeboxes and record players "lifesaving machines"[25] because of rock's role in preserving his own identity, connects himself closely to the music as to other aspects of the film. The first time a jukebox appears in *Alice*, in a South Carolinian roadside cafe, Wenders is recognizable as the young man in the background playing it. In an ice cream parlor in Wuppertal, a small boy sits next to a jukebox listening to Canned Heat's "On the Road Again." Probably he is Wenders' image of himself as a youngster, for Wenders later said: "The first thing which was really important to me was sitting, listening to Chuck Berry on a jukebox, in a place where I was not allowed to go"[26] (probably *not* an ice cream parlor). Later Philip goes to the concert where Chuck Berry is accompanied by Canned Heat.

A film for which the crew journeyed through two continents, *Alice* was intended as the quintessential film about travel. Out of 110 minutes total running time, approximately 24 minutes (21 percent) show the characters in or looking out of moving vehicles. Wenders tried to include every possible mode of modern transportation: car, subway, bus, airplane, motorboat, bicycle, ferry, and train. The only reason he sent his characters to Wuppertal was to photograph them on Wuppertal's *Schwebebahn* (suspended railway), unique in Germany. *Alice* is the only Wenders film to include a close-up of a road map.

Travel, of course, is a metaphor for the search for identity. For Wenders, travel is literally a means of discovering one's identity. "Foreignness . . . is just a throughway to a notion of identity. . . . And I think everybody's senses are more aware when they're travelling. . . . "[27] Travelling to discover one's identity has a long history in German culture, for it forms the basis of the *Bildungsroman*, the German literary genre in which a young man travels to find his true being and purpose in life. The tradition began in the eighteenth century with Goethe's *Wilhelm Meister's Apprenticeship* (*Wilhelm Meisters Lehrjahre*) and continued into the twentieth century. Wenders' next film *Wrong Move* (*Falsche Bewegung,* 1975) was loosely based on the Goethe novel and, with Rüdiger Vogler as the lead, continued to explore the angst of the postwar generation.

With its emphasis on driving sequences and the documenting of phenomena, *Alice* returned to the style Wenders began developing while still in film school. The painterly contrasts of light and dark in *Alabama* and *Summer* were further refined in *Alice*, where Müller played with the elusive feathery reflections of trees on the car windshield and insubstantial portraits of Alice observed through panes of glass.

Wenders' themes developed, too. From the mute heroes of *Alabama* and *Summer* and the paralyzed goalie, Wenders created a protagonist capable of growth and change. Travel was no longer an escape, but a search. From the general notion of recording phenomena and from his enthusiasm for rock music, Wenders began to develop and represent a specific philosophy that related hearing and seeing to identity and personal growth. To these he linked children and eventually filmmaking. A complex philosophy rooted at one end in *sensibilisten* concerns, it would broaden and deepen in *Kings of the Road* and *The American Friend*.

5

Road Movies:
Wrong Move and *Kings of the Road*

In 1975 Wenders formed a production company in Berlin called Road Movies in honor of the most salient feature in his work, the restless travelling men "at home in no house and in no country. . . ."[1] Though nearly all of Wenders' films touched on this theme to some extent, three in particular came to epitomize it: *Alice in the Cities, Wrong Move,* and *Kings of the Road,* all starring Rüdiger Vogler as the disaffected hero.

Wrong Move was made from a script by Peter Handke based loosely on Goethe's classic *Bildungsroman Wilhelm Meister's Apprenticeship,* and thus became Wenders' second major collaboration with Handke. In the Goethe novel, Wilhelm is the son of a bourgeois businessman, loves the actress Mariane but, fearing she has been unfaithful, abandons her to take up his father's profession. He is, nevertheless, lured away by a troupe of travelling players which include the flirtatious Philine and the cynical Laertes. A slightly deranged harper, burdened by a secret past, joins them as does Mignon, an abused child Wilhelm buys from a ropewalker in a travelling circus. Usually mute, Mignon finds comfort in the company of the harper and at the same time becomes fiercely attached to Wilhelm. Later in the story the reader is led to believe that Wilhelm has mistakenly made love to Mignon, though eventually this proves untrue.

The actors stay for a time at the court of a local count and perform for him. There they meet and mock a baron who fancies himself a poet. Wilhelm becomes infatuated with the count's beautiful wife and nearly compromises her honor. In extricating himself he pretends to be a ghost and frightens the count so badly that the latter becomes a religious fanatic. Soon after this incident the troupe leaves the court only to be ambushed and robbed. While Wilhelm convalesces, the troupe disintegrates; eventually Wilhelm, taking Mignon and the harper, joins the troupe of Serlo. There, through a series of coincidences typical of eighteenth-century novels, Wilhelm discovers that his first love Mariane, now dead, was never untrue to him and bore him a child named Felix, whom Serlo's sister Aurelie took into custody.

Aurelie dies and leaves Wilhelm with his child and a letter for her former lover Lothario, a utopianist inspired by a sojourn in America to create an ideal community on his lands. Lothario also happens to be the brother of the beautiful countess, whose husband Wilhelm had frightened. A second sister, the compassionate Natalie, captures Wilhem's heart and eventually marries him—after Wilhelm disentangles himself from an engagement to the level-headed Therese, who is really in love with Lothario. In the meantime Wilhelm has been inducted into the Society of the Tower through which Lothario's former tutor, the Abbé, directs the fates of young men in order to guide them into self-realization. Despite his recent nuptials, Wilhelm is directed to continue his travels and the novel ends with Wilhelm still on his quest for self-realization. Before he leaves, Mignon dies, the harper commits suicide, and Wilhelm finally learns their histories. The harper had unknowingly married his own sister, and Mignon was the child of their incestuous union.

Peter Handke had already explored the *Bildungsroman* genre in his *Short Letter, Long Farewell,* in which the narrator–hero travels across America trying to come to terms with a broken marriage. Anxious that the reader recognize the genre he was working in, Handke had his hero read Gottfried Keller's *Green Henry*, a *Bildungsroman* from 1854. In *Wrong Move* the hero's mother gives him a copy of Joseph von Eichendorff's *Memoirs of a Good-for-Nothing,* another nineteenth-century *Bildungsroman.*

Handke's adaptation of Goethe retains Wilhelm Meister as the young man setting out to find his calling, as well as some names and vague parallels to situations in Goethe's novel. The film begins with a helicopter panorama of Glückstadt, a small town in Schleswig-Holstein on the Elbe halfway between Hamburg and the North Sea. Wilhelm Meister (Rüdiger Vogler), son of a petit-bourgeois widow, stares out of his bedroom window at the town square below. Suddenly he thrusts his first through the window. His mother (Marianne Hoppe) appears at the door. She says nothing about the broken window, but, in the sonambulist manner of so many Handke characters, tells Wilhelm that he ought to leave home and travel throughout Germany to fulfill his ambition of becoming a writer. Wilhelm bids his frumpy hometown girlfriend (Lisa Kreuzer) good-bye and entrains for Bonn. Two vagabonds join him, a cynical, harmonica-playing ex-Nazi named Laertes (Hans Christian Blech) and his companion, the mute, theatrically trained teenager Mignon (Nastassja Kinski in her first screen appearance). Changing trains in Hamburg, Wilhelm spots a woman (Hanna Schygulla) on a neighboring train and stares after her. Laertes informs him that she is the actress Therese Farner, and soon the conductor appears with her telephone number, which she has wired to Wilhelm. Wilhelm telephones her from Bonn, and she appears the next day. Accompanied by Laertes and Mignon, Wilhelm and Therese set off on a walk. Bernhard Landau (Peter Kern), a wealthy would-be poet, joins them. He suggests they visit his wealthy uncle, but mistakes the estate, and the five stumble in on a wealthy industrialist (Ivan Desny) on the verge of suicide. Suffering from accute loneliness, his

Wrong Move (1975)
Laertes (Hans Christian Blech), Mignon (Nastassja Kinski), Wilhelm (Rüdiger Vogler), and Therese (Hanna Schygulla) set out for a walk.
(Courtesy Gray City, Inc.)

wife having committed suicide several months earlier, the industrialist invites them to stay. He delivers a disquisition on loneliness and fear in Germany.

> Here, fear is either vanity or shame. That's why loneliness in Germany hides behind all these faithless, soulless faces that haunt the supermarkets, public gardens, shopping centers, and health clubs. The dead souls of Germany!

Therese invites Wilhelm to sleep with her, but he mistakes her room for Mignon's and sleeps with the teenager instead. In the morning they discuss the dreams that each has supposedly had during the night and then climb the nearby hills overlooking the Rhine. Laertes reveals his guilty secret to Wilhelm: he used to command the concentration camp at Wilna; Wilhelm privately resolves to kill him. Caught by an impulse to run back down the hill, the five arrive at the house out-of-breath to find that the indusrtrialist has hanged himself. Leaving quickly, they travel to Therese's home in Frankfurt, losing Bernhard on the way. Therese and Wilhelm fight, and Wilhelm admits to himself, "I couldn't help Therese and had hidden behind my work although I knew very well that I couldn't call it work if I wasn't at the same time, open to Therese."

Unable to satisfy Therese, Wilhelm decides to leave, but not before killing Laertes. During a ferryboat ride he threatens to throw the old man overboard, but Laertes begs for mercy, and Wilhelm lets him go. Mignon elects to stay with Therese, and Wilhelm sets off alone to visit the Zugspitze, Germany's highest mountain. Here another Bildungsroman, Thomas Mann's *The Magic Mountain*, is invoked as Wilhelm stands at the top of the Zugspitze looking out. He muses:

> Why did I flee, why was I here instead of with the others? Why had I threatened the old man instead of letting him tell me more? It seemed to me as if I had missed something, as if I always missed something with every new move.

The superficial similarities between Goethe's novel and Handke's screenplay are obvious. The name of the hero has been retained, and other names have been borrowed from the novel and used for characters with at least a vague similarity to their forerunners. The mad harper with a guilty past becomes Handke's harmonica-playing Laertes, whose name, however, comes from Goethe's cynical actor. Handke's Therese is also a composite. She is an actress like Goethe's Mariane but goes about her affairs with a deliberateness that originates in his Therese. Like Natalie, Handke's Therese is left behind when Wilhelm recommences his travels at the end of the story; otherwise she little resembles Goethe's near-perfect heroine. Mignon resembles her namesake most closely: an androgynous child with a mysterious past, theatrically trained, silent, and strongly attached to Wilhelm. Handke cynically transforms the episode in which Goethe lets us believe that Wilhelm has inadvertently slept with Mignon and has his Wilhelm, at first mistaking Mignon's room for Therese's, knowingly stay and make love to the young girl.

Bernhard Landau probably derives from the baron who writes bad verse, and the industrialist who commits suicide from Goethe's count who becomes a religious fanatic after Wilhelm frightens him. The disintegration of Handke's group after the industrialist's death parallels the ambush and consequent disintegration of the troupe after they leave the count's court. The episodes in Frankfurt are the counterpart of the utopian experiment on Lothario's estate.

Of the *Bildungsroman,* Martin Swales writes, "The lifeblood of the genre is consistently sustained irresolution." About *Wilhelm Meister* in particular he writes:

> Wilhelm really does not know all the answers by the end. . . . A mere three pages from the end of the novel, Wilhelm laments his inadequacy and wonders whether he will ever be able to assume proper control of his life: "Again have my eyes been opened to my conduct; but it was always too late, always in vain!"
> . . . Ultimately, the novel comes to rest on an article of faith: the world gives the individual the room and the time to grow as his selfhood demands. . . . In one sense then, there is a happy ending, but it is perfunctory because the process of living and erring goes on.[2]

The major elements of the *Bildungsroman,* the journey in search of oneself, the failures and self-recriminations, the lack of resolution, are all present in *Wrong Move* and tie it firmly to this tradition. Both Wilhelms feel that they have been insensitive and have failed the people they should have helped, and both leave for further travels at the unresolved end. Nevertheless *Wrong Move*, in contrast to Handke's *Short Letter, Long Farewell*, has a deliberately anti-Bildungsroman undercurrent. Overlain with Handke's cynicism, *Wrong Move* portrays a paralysis in its hero similar to the goalie's. Goethe's Wilhelm loves and is able to respond to people where Handke's Wilhelm does not and cannot. Goethe's Wilhelm is active; Handke's is passive. Handke's Wilhelm does not actively cause other people to suffer; he is not responsible for the industrialist's suicide while Goethe's Wilhelm *is* responsible for the count's becoming a religious fanatic. Handke's Wilhelm deliberately insults his hometown girlfriend, but he does not misjudge and mistrust her or leave her pregnant and destitute as Goethe's Wilhelm does Mariane. Handke's Wilhelm tries to kill Laertes but gives up even this one attempt at action. He lacks sins of commission, which corresponds to his lack of zeal and passion, the qualities which endear Goethe's Wilhelm to the reader despite his many failures.

Both men leave for further travels at the end, but Goethe's Wilhelm leaves at the urging of the Abbé and others concerned for his further education. Handke's Wilhelm leaves to escape attachment to a woman and acknowledges that further travels won't bring him what he really needs.

> I had told Therese that I . . . still knew too little about Germany to be able to write about it. But that was just an excuse. In reality I just wanted to be alone, to remain undisturbed in my insensitivity. I stood on the Zugspitze and waited for something to happen as though I were waiting for a miracle. But the snowstorm didn't come.

Having already withdrawn from the "storm," an active engagement with life, Wilhelm waits for a storm he can passively observe, but finally acknowledges that this stance will only cause him to miss out on life "with every new move." *Wrong Move* deliberately subverts elements of the *Bildungsroman* tradition by sending a young man on educative travels who is, in terms of the education these travels offer, virtually ineducable.

Eric Rentschler has raised the question of whether Handke or Wenders is responsible for subverting the *Bildungsroman* genre in *Wrong Move*.[3] Handke's original script, published by Suhrkamp Verlag, ends differently from the film. In it we don't actually see Wilhelm on the Zugspitze; instead a shot of him leaving Frankfurt dissolves into a view of the Zugspitze in a snowstorm. Over the sound of the storm, the sound of a typewriter becomes louder and louder. Earlier in this script Wilhelm tells Therese, "I want to walk around in a snowstorm. That's why I'm leaving: so I'll understand why I'm so discontented. When I'm alone, I'll be able to remember, especially you, and when I can remember again, I'll feel well and feel like writing."[4] Thus in the original script Wilhelm's flight from the group is justified: he foresees that it will allow him to become a writer, and it does.

In the film, however, Wilhelm ends as he began: disliking people, alone, and, because of his isolation, still far from achieving his goal. Thus the finished film takes a 180° turn philosophically from the original script. According to Wenders, Handke wrote the script in Venice and sent it to him. Presumably this is the script Handke published, for it concludes with the inscription "*Venedig, Juli/August 1973*" (Venice, July/August 1973).[5] Wenders rewrote the script with a shot breakdown and sent it back. Handke made more changes, and Wenders filmed this revised script. He maintains he was completely faithful to this version. "I changed a lot of the locations and looks, but none of the dialogue was changed at all."[6] When it became clear that the script as written would be too long, voice-overs were added to cut down on the amount of dialogue, and Handke wrote these voice-overs, which include Wilhelm's final monologue on the Zugspitze. Clearly then, Handke authored the film's words. Rentschler is probably right, however, in assuming that the changed view of Wilhelm's isolationism from positive to negative is Wenders' contribution since in *Alice* and in *Kings* the characters progress—for example, Philip Winter is able to write again—only when they renounce their isolation in favor of human interaction. Wenders comments sourly on Wilhelm, however: "Wilhelm is no longer a hero at the end . . . not even in his own eyes. He could become a human being. But that would be another film."[7]

Shooting *Wrong Move* required the same precise approach that Wenders used for *Goalie*. "*Wrong Move* comes from someone for whom language was very important and was the theme of the film: how to be able to grasp the world through language. That's why in this film I was very faithful to the text."[8] Yet Wenders' translation of Handke's words into images is often brilliant. In several instances Wilhelm acknowledges his ability to deal with people and feelings only by remembering them. Over a driving sequence he says,

> Sometimes I stared straight ahead for a long time purposely not looking at anything. Then I closed my eyes and only then, from the after-image that was produced thereby, did I notice what had been in front of me.

In the following shot we see a picture window at night in Therese's apartment in which the people in her living room are reflected. The window visualizes Wilhelm's words about the "after-image" and his tendency to deal with people only at a remove.

Judges at the 1975 Berlin Film Festival responded favorably to the film's cool precision and awarded it seven *Bundesfilm* prizes: best film, director, screenplay, editing, music, cinematography, and cast. Including the shorts, it was Peter Handke's third film with Wenders, Jürgen Knieper's fourth, Peter Przygodda's fifth, and Robbie Müller's sixth. Of the cast Hans Christian Blech had worked with Wenders once previously, Lisa Kreuzer twice, and Rüdiger Vogler three times. The teamwork on which Wenders' films depend was recognized and awarded by the Festival judges. A man who does not work well under others, Wenders nevertheless inspires great commitment from those who work under him. Such commitment alone made his next film possible.

Despite the kudos, Wenders was impatient to return to a more spontaneous approach to filmmaking. "*Wrong Move*," he said "had a static script and had to be a static film. But for me personally, this requirement got on my nerves."[9] The restrictions of *Wrong Move* gave birth to a concept for a freer film. "There were a lot of things that I would have liked to film, but I couldn't. I therefore got the idea for a film which follows an itinerary but where there would always be the possibility of using whatever we saw during the actual shooting."[10]

Kings of the Road (*Im Lauf der Zeit,* 1976) began as an itinerary of small towns with extant movie theaters along the border between East and West Germany. The story was to be that of an itinerant movie projector repairman travelling in a made-over moving van. Putting his own money (Wim Wenders Produktion) into the film, Wenders went on location with only the itinerary, a few pages of script, the van, the principle actors, and the team. Every night he wrote dialogue until early morning, and when the ideas wouldn't come, the team didn't shoot the next day.

The story that evolved in this way was that of Bruno Winter (Rüdiger Vogler), a loner who travels up and down West Germany's border with the East, fixing the projectors in provincial movie houses. The film begins, however, with Robert Lander (Hanns Zischler), a child psychologist specializing in language disorders and recently separated from his wife, driving his Volkswagen beetle along provincial roads. His progress is intercut with Bruno's morning ritual at his campsite beside the Elbe. Suddenly Robert's car appears, and Bruno watches with amazement as Robert drives straight into the river. Abandoning his sinking car, Robert swims to shore, where Bruno meets him. Unused to the idea of friendship, the two travel together awkwardly and a little desperately. Camped in an abandoned basalt mine

Kings of the Road (1976)
Bruno (Rüdiger Vogler) watches Robert escape the sinking car.
(*Courtesy Road Movies*)

Kings of the Road (1976)
Robert "Kamikaze" Lander (Hanns Zischler) after escaping his sinking car.
(Courtesy Gray City, Inc.)

they meet a man (Marquard Bohm) whose wife committed suicide the day before by driving into a tree.

Promising to catch up with Bruno, Robert leaves to visit his father (Rudolf Schündler), who runs a newspaper in one of the small towns. He berates his father for having been too domineering, but finally lets the old man sleep while he sets up his complaints in type. Meanwhile Bruno has picked up a woman, Pauline (Lisa Kreuzer), at a midway in another small town and invites her to a show. She accepts, but when Bruno goes to the theater to meet her, he finds she already works there (helping out her grandmother). They spend a chaste night together unable to break out of their mutual isolation. In the morning Bruno stops by the newspaper office to pick up Robert. They decide to visit Bruno's childhood home, an old house on an island in the Rhine, and borrow an old BMW motorcycle with sidecar from a friend of Robert's. They travel across West Germany to the Rhine and row out to the island. The house is abandoned. Bruno explores it briefly and then sits down and weeps. In the morning they drive back and continue with Bruno's itinerary.

One evening they dead-end at the border and spend the night in an abandoned U.S. Army patrol hut. Discussing the absence of women in their lives they tacitly recognize the limits of male friendship. The next morning Robert leaves without waking Bruno; a one-sentence note explains his disappearance. "Everything must change," he writes. Bruno is hurt, but in the end accepts Robert's challenge. He makes one more stop then tears up his itinerary.

Kings is thus a more straightforward treatment of the Bildungsroman tradition than is *Wrong Move*. Like *Alice*'s Philip, the men in *Kings* show a capacity for growth and change by the end of the film.

Images of circle and cycle pervade the film. The men's friendship begins when Robert emerges soaking wet at the edge of the river having climbed out of the narrow opening atop his womb-like Volkswagen, and it ends when they reach a *dead* end, the patrol hut on the East German border. Between these references to the life cycle, images and references to circles indicate the entrapment, the resistance to change, that Robert feels needs escaping. Unlike other travellers in Wenders' films, Bruno travels in a circuit, of which the big wheels on his truck serve to remind us. Robert accuses him of living in a snail shell (*Schneckenhaus*). Robert himself rides a bicycle around in circles inside a small courtyard and later plays with a hula hoop. He relates his dream of always having to write in a circle (until he discovers a new ink). At the midway, Pauline's bumper car ride takes her in a circle and later Bruno splices together a loop film to show in her theater. Finding a way out of this overarching circle is the problem posed by the film. When Robert visits his father and when he and Bruno leave the van to travel to the Rhine on the motorcycle, they break the circle and by doing so come to know more of their personal histories. The circle is equated to the dead end the men come to when they reach the East German border, an equation not as absurd as it sounds if one considers that death is not simply an end but part of a cycle—the begining of which we have already seen in Robert's "birth." In the patrol hut Robert tells Bruno, "You're as good as dead!" and later insists, "You can't go on living like this, if you can't imagine anything else or don't even want to change." Subsequently both men break out of the circle: Robert leaves Bruno and his circuit and takes the train while Bruno acknowledges his intention of abandoning the circuit by tearing up his itinerary.

Of all Wenders' films, *Kings* has the closest ties to documentary. After deciding the route his protagonist would take along the border, Wenders made several trips to the area to investigate local movie houses and interview their owners. The film begins and ends with Bruno interviewing theater owners, the first an old man who used to play the violin for silent films, the second an old woman, an actress rather than a real owner, whose dialogue nevertheless was based on the sentiments of numerous owners that Wenders had interviewed.

In *Kings* Wenders laid bare the situation he had first become aware of while working for United Artists ten years earlier, the exploitation of provincial movie houses by commercial film distributors.

> Most of these village movie theaters belong to old women who run them with a real obsession, even at a loss. They all knew that they had no successors and that the theaters in the countryside are going to die with them.[11]

The opening interview is one of many Wenders filmed with real theater owners. He discarded the others because their insertion disrupted the fragile storyline too much. Nevertheless the dismal view we get of the provincial theaters throughout the film, whose fare we sample in Pauline's theater, serves to document their distress.

Stylistically *Kings* and *Wrong Move* vary somewhat, primarily because they were conceived of differently. "I think," Wenders said, "black-and-white is much more realistic and natural than color. . . . I would never, ever, shoot a documentary in color."[12] Although Wenders considers all films documents of some sort, clearly the black-and-white *Kings* was intended as such more than *Wrong Move*, a color film. Wenders' open-ended approach to the *Kings'* script allowed him to incorporate whatever he noticed of interest along his route.

Like *Alice*, *Kings* incorporates a great many driving sequences, twice as many per foot of film as *Wrong Move*. (At 12 percent and 6 percent, respectively, both films have fewer than *Alice* at 21 percent.)

Wrong Move, on the other hand, emphasizes objects as did *Goalie*. In the industrialist's living room everything is wrapped in plastic, ostensibly because he is renovating. When one notices, however, that the television set is turned on and playing under its plastic wrap, the other wrapped objects in the room begin to stand out as *objects* (reminiscent of Christo's art) rather than merely as furnishings in a room being renovated. Although the obsession with objects is Handkean, the idea of wrapping them is Wenders'. He first used wrapped objects in the lost short

Schauplätze and would use them again in *American Friend*, where many of the artifacts in Ripley's living room are wrapped in plastic on the excuse that he is an amateur painter.

Rhythm and cutting differ considerably between *Wrong Move* and *Kings*. While the pace of the action in both films is slow, the cutting in *Wrong Move* is often disjunctive and abrupt, while *Kings* cultivates a comforting leisureliness derived from the Hollywood western.

As a critic, Wenders often praised films for their leisureliness. "In *Red Sun* people just talk on as if the progress of the film had nothing to do with them," he wrote.[13] Of Raoul Walsh's *The Tall Men:*

> When Jane Russell starts to get dressed and Clark Gable meanwhile takes care of his horse outside and then dreamily listens to her singing, one readily believes, as she calls him in and, as he comes into the room, buttons the last button on her dress, that the film has given her enough time to get dressed.[14]

After *Goalie* he told a reporter, "No matter what kind of film it is, I find it important that a loyalty be there toward the passage of time. . . ."[15] Thus in *Kings*, Robert leaves a car he has hitched a ride in and walks to Bruno sitting in the cab of the truck. We wait with Bruno, who fiddles with objects in the cab until Robert has actually had time to reach the truck. In another instance we wait with Bruno for a train to pass so that he can cross the railroad tracks. Unlike the sequence at the end during which he waits for *Robert's* train to pass and comments the while, this scene has no other significance than to show us the train and let us live the time passing.

Throughout *Kings* Wenders inserts a dawn landscape between scenes of characters going to sleep at night and then awakening in the morning. Again the salient influence is the American western. In his *Tall Men* review he noted,

> Because of a snowstorm, Clark Gable and Jane Russell have to stop over in an abandoned log cabin. The snowstorm only needed to last one day in order to allow the conflict between the two . . . to break out. But it lasts two days, and the new day is established each time by a panorama shot.[16]

Likewise Wenders doesn't *need* to show the dawn landscapes in *Kings* just to indicate that morning has come on three separate days; rather he wants to show the passage of time. Such literal indication of the passage of time bears on the theme of the film, which, reflecting on personal history and time passed, is summed up in the film's German title *Im Lauf der Zeit* ("In the Course of Time").

The unhurried attitude is taken up by the characters in *Kings* as well. When the man whose wife has committed suicide asks to remain in the truck until his wife's smashed car is towed away, Robert denies his request, telling the man that he and Bruno must move on. But Bruno contradicts him. "No," he says, "we don't have to move on." And they stay. The sequence is reminiscent of Philip's remark to Alice when finding Grandmother's house still doesn't produce Grandmother. "Then we can go swimming after all," he tells her. For the audience that can hold out against the lack of action, the feeling that neither the director nor the characters are urging the film forward lends greater credibility to the characters. James Monaco writes of *Kings*, "Something psychologically interesting happens after two hours of film time: audiences gradually stop looking at the characters on the screen and start living with them."[17]

In *Wrong Move*, as in *Goalie*, precision, dictated by the precision of Handke's prose, replaces leisureliness. Moreover the cutting frequently frustrates the viewer by occurring just before an action is completed or too long after, as though forcing the skewed and alienated perspective of the protagonist on the viewer. For example, when Wilhelm's train passes a station, the camera holds on the station platform and its clock. The second hands on such clocks stop momentarily at the end of each minute to allow the minute hand to move forward. The shot cuts just before the minute hand springs forward and gives the impression that the clock has stopped. Likewise when Therese telephones Wilhelm in Bonn, the phone rings repeatedly. Just as Wilhelm goes to pick it up, the shot cuts and disappoints our expectation of hearing the phone answered and the ringing silenced. On the other hand, when the group runs down an alley and around the corner, Bernhard tries to follow, loses the group, then follows it around the corner. The camera does not follow him, however, and continues to film the empty path. When Wilhelm gets up to go to bed at the industrialist's house, the camera holds on his empty chair. When the group leaves the industrialist's house, the camera holds on the empty doorway. The little disappointments set up by the editing prepare the audience for the larger ones in the story: Wilhelm Meister sets out to discover life and love but manages to elude both.

Handke's influence on the pace of *Wrong Move* may have been more than literary. Handke made a film for television in 1970 called *Chronik der laufenden Ereignisse* ("Chronicle of Current Events"), an impressionistic account, according to Handke, of West German television during 1968 and 1969. The film includes several shots of the clock which appears on German television and gongs on the hour. In one of these shots the clock "forgets" to gong. In another shot a man (Rüdiger Vogler) places a telephone call, and the film cuts immediately to a telephone that we can only suppose is the one being called: it doesn't ring. The clock that doesn't gong and the telephone that doesn't ring in *Chronik*, although created by manipulating the sound track, are similar in impact to the clock that appears to stop and the telephone that won't stop ringing in *Wrong Move*, impressions created by the editing. Since Handke also helped edit *Wrong Move*, he may well have contributed the idea of cutting before the clock's hand sprang forward and before the telephone was answered.

Acting style also differs between *Wrong Move* and *Kings*. Beginning with *Alice*, Wenders explored the possibility of using gesture as a communication device rather than speech. He was probably influenced by Ozu in this since he first saw Ozu's films while writing the script for *Alice* and since Ozu's characters have such a rich repertoire of comic, earthy, and sympathetic gestures. In *Kings*, where the characters say little to one another, gesture is a primary means of communication. The opening sequence, in which Robert and Bruno meet, contains two lines of dialogue. Parked on the bank of the Elbe and shaving inside the cab of his truck, Bruno watches bemused, looks away in disbelief, doubles up with laughter, and scratches his chin with concern as Robert drives into the river and then tries to escape the sinking car. Bruno puts down his shaving brush, gets out of the truck, and knocks his shaving cup off the car window ledge. He picks up the shaving equipment while wiping cream off his chin and watches Robert, who is making his way to shore. Bruno meets him as he wades out of the river, and they laugh. Bruno nods his head toward the truck. At the truck Robert glares at Bruno, sits down, and hugs his knees. Bruno drops a towel over Robert's shoulders; Robert wipes his head, then weeps into the towel. Bruno brings him the rest of his coffee from the cab. In the entire sequence the only lines of dialogue are Robert's noting that his shoes squeak and Bruno's offering him dry clothes. The characters of Robert and Bruno and the advent of their relationship are thus mapped out without dialogue. Later the pantomime that Robert and Bruno spontaneously stage for a group of school children celebrates the art of gesture while its slapstick comedy recalls silent films.

By contrast, the acting in *Wrong Move* is centered on the dialogue, which is delivered in a stilted, formal manner, meant to conjure up an earlier century for the viewer. Only the mute Mignon relies on gesture, but even these seem overly deliberate and lack the spontaneity of the gestures in *Alice* and *Kings*.

Thus the trilogy of *Alice*, *Wrong Move*, and *Kings*, unified by Rüdiger Volger's persona and by the fact that all three combine the American road movie genre with that of the German *Bildungsroman,* nevertheless lacks stylistic and philosophical unity. In conception, shooting, acting, and editing *Alice* and *Kings* are spontaneous, documentary, unhurried, and hopeful, while *Wrong Move* is static, precise, literary, disjunctive, and pessimistic.

Many of the themes Wenders had pursued since *Summer* culminate in *Wrong Move* and *Kings*. He continued to explore means of communication: rock music, film, and language. "My life was saved by rock 'n roll," reads some graffitti in *Kings'* hut on the border, and indeed rock and roll is again treated as a purely positive, free, joyous, unproblematic means of communication. Bruno carries an entire jukebox in the back of his truck and keeps an archaic battery-operated 45 record player in his cab. After the trip to the Rhine, Bruno pops Heinz' "Just Like Eddie" into the 45 player, and he and Robert sing along, marking the high point of their friendship.

If true communication takes place for Wenders' characters through the agency of rock and roll, it rarely takes place through the agency of language. In *Wrong Move* the characters discourse excessively in what one reviewer calls "a vaguely nineteenth-century language with which one never feels comfortable."[18] The

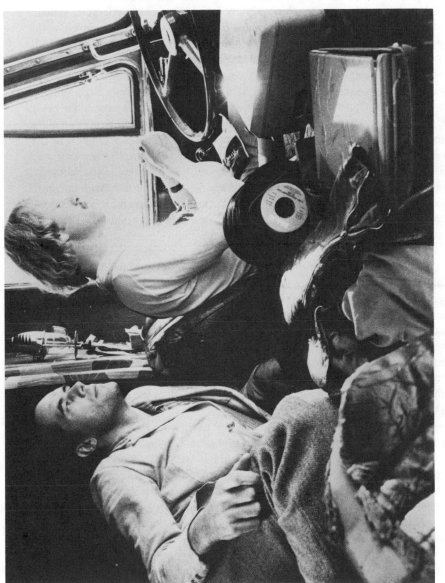

Kings of the Road (1976)
Robert and Bruno sing "Just like Eddie."
(Courtesy Gray City, Inc.)

speeches are rarely conversational but always in the form of short essays or literary dialogues. Twice in the Frankfurt section of the film Hanna Schuygulla as Therese fluffs a line ever so slightly. Wenders' use of these takes underscores the idea that she is making a speech not simply conversing. Every character remains isolated behind a screen of literary formulations through which he or she apparently hopes to deal with but not be touched by other human beings. Even Therese, who so actively seeks contact with Wilhelm, is caught behind this veil. When Wilhelm "accidentally" sleeps with Mignon, Therese does not confront him with her feelings directly but invents a dream of coldness, isolation, and rejection, a kind of prose poem, and tells it to the group. When Wilhelm finally pushes her to the breaking point, she threatens to bash his head in with an iron, but she is still unable to express her feelings with language. When, at the end, Wilhelm asks her how they should part, she answers dramatically, "Somewhere in the throng." When they reach the sparsely populated shopping center, he teases, "Well, where is your throng?" Therese can dramatize and poeticize, but she cannot communicate with language. Likewise the industrialist speaks eloquently, but can't overcome his loneliness. Wilhelm and Laertes discourse on politics but don't seem to reach one another. Throughout, Mignon's silence comments on the empty, pompous speeches.

The idea that literary formulations block true communication is carried further in the character of Wilhelm. "Wilhelm wants to become a writer," says Wenders, "and is always trying to connect with people in terms of language, so he never gets at that contact he needs."[19] In moments of self-scrutiny Wilhelm questions his desire to write in the face of his inability to deal with people. "I want to become a writer," he muses at the beginning of the film, "but how is that possible when I have no joy in people?" He tells Laertes, "Politics first became incomprehensible to me when I started writing." And later he reproves himself for hiding behind his writing when he couldn't help Therese. Writing distances Wilhelm from human society just as their literary speeches distance all of the characters from one another.

Kings contains little spoken dialogue, but as the son of a newspaperman and specialist in children's linguistics, Robert is associated with language. Language is a positive force in *Kings*, however, and as such is frequently associated with children. In one town Robert finds children sailing paper boats made of newspaper. He unfolds one and sits near them to read it. Having grown up with the newspaper, he tells his father, "The whole time I've been gone, whenever I think or say something I immediately see it printed." He carries this tendency out literally when, unable to explain to his father his feelings about how women should be treated, he sets them in print and runs a copy. A special edition is not perhaps an ideal solution to communication barriers, but in this film it is a beginning.

Later Robert explains to Bruno that writing is at first an adventure for children: "There was a boy—the lines were roads for him on which the letters rode with the help of a motorcycle, the pen." Freshness and adventure, a natural stance for children, facilitate communication. Robert also dreams about writing, and here too Wenders stresses the need for a fresh approach.

> There used to be an ink with which you could erase old writing and at the same time write something new. I always had to think and write down the same thing, again and again, even if I woke up out of the dream once in a while. Dreaming was writing in a circle till I had the idea in the dream to use another kind of ink, the new kind, and with the new kind I could suddenly think and see something new and write. Everything solved itself.

The ability to "think and write something new," is again the child's view. At the end of the film Robert meets a boy who is writing down everything he sees. "As simple as that?" asks Robert after the boy has described the project to him. "As simple as that," replies the boy. As with hearing and seeing, only a return to the values of childhood facilitates communication in Wenders' view. Writing can block or be blocked or it can break down barriers and express something new depending on the disposition of the writer.

Film as a source of communication is more problematic than writing. Wenders alludes to the range of possibilities in *Wrong Move:* Coppola's *Conversation* plays on the town square in Bonn; Straub and Huillet's *Chronicle of Anna Magdalena Bach* plays on television in Frankfurt; and Peter Lilienthal's *La Victoria* appears, improbably, at a drive-in theater. *Wrong Move* thus gives a nod to the American independent cinema and the New German Cinema, much as *Goalie* and *Alice* celebrated the American genre films of Siegel, Hawks, and Ford. At the other end of the spectrum is Wilhelm's hometown movie house, which is playing *The Return of the Mounted Corpses*, a third-rate horror film from Spain.[20] The title no doubt reminded Wenders of one of the first films he had seen as a child, *The Night of the Mounted Corpses*, which made a lasting impression,[21] but it also reflects the pathetic fare available at provincial movie houses. *Kings* would continue this story.

At the end of *Kings* Bruno speaks to an old woman who has closed her theater but who keeps her projection equipment repaired in case she might want to use it. She tells him:

> My father used to say that film is the art of seeing, and that's why I can't show these pictures that exploit anything that is left to exploit from people's eyes and minds, where people stumble out benumbed by stupidity, that destroy their very lust for life. . . .

Pauline's theater, where a porno feature is playing, has already proved the woman's point. Neglecting his duties, the projectionist masturbates while watching the film. Bruno scares him off and proceeds to make a loop of the snarled film the projectionist has left on the floor. "Violence, sex, action! Ninety minutes of film you won't see on television," chants the narration as three 30-second shots follow one another over and over: a burning house, a rape scene, and a naked woman's heaving breasts. Pauline recalls that a former patron, actively participating in the pleasures depicted on the screen, suffered a vaginal cramp and had to be carried out with her boyfriend still inside her. Added to Bruno's discovery of the masturbating projectionist, Pauline's story indicates the degree of vulgarity porno films elicit. They have the opposite effect on Bruno and Pauline, however, whose shyness and hesitancy is heightened by the pornographic display. The exploitation of sex on the screen chills their own undernurtured sense of intimacy, and each returns to his/her semi-isolation—"semi" because Pauline has a child and Bruno has Robert. Wenders thus links the misuse of film with another of his recurrent themes, the failure of communication between men and women.

In *Wrong Move* Wilhelm's mother gives him two books to take on his trip, Eichendorff's *Memoirs of a Good-for-Nothing* and Flaubert's *Sentimental Education*. Ironically both involve heroes who are smitten by ideal heroines and strive ceaselessly to win them. The traditionally romantic prelude to *Wrong Move*'s love story—the lovers spying each other from passing trains (preceded by a close shot of two cars on the train being coupled)—is not followed up in the subsequent story. The Bildungroman's romantic tradition is inverted by Therese's ceaseless striving to win the cold and reluctant Wilhelm. Wilhelm, on the other hand, is convinced he could love Therese if he just weren't around her. He has similar feelings about his mother: "Later, somewhere else . . . I would be able to remember her better." Like his mother, Therese senses he will leave her and makes no move to stop him. The relationship Wilhelm flees has been neither happy nor unhappy; it simply hasn't happened.

In one sense *Kings* begins where *Wrong Move* leaves off. Robert and Bruno have tried to escape from women: Bruno by encapsulating himself in his truck and Robert by fleeing his marriage. Yet absent women haunt both the escapees and the film. Robert tries constantly to call his estranged wife. Usually she hangs up. He berates his father for mistreating his mother, who died eight years earlier, but is moved when his father confesses that he never knew his own mother, who died at his birth. Bruno, who grew up with only a mother, finds his childhood home empty when he returns to it. The third man they meet has lost his wife in a suicidal car accident.

The yearning for women produces various reactions in the men. Bruno suppresses his desire with scorn. He refers to wanting women as being "*in der Tinte*," literally "in the ink," meaning "up the creek." When Robert relates his dream of finding the new ink that solved the problem of writing in circles, Bruno replies, "You're still 'in the ink,'" referring to Robert's attempts to call his wife. When Pauline, waiting for Bruno's advances, asks, "What now?" he replies, "Now I'm 'in the ink.'" In another scene she stands inside the doorway to the projection booth and asks Bruno if he plans to spend the night. He nods in the affirmative, but the shot of Pauline shows her standing next to a wall telephone whose cord is tied into a noose, a *subjective* correlative for Bruno's fear of women. Relationships in general and sex in particular are so threatening to Bruno that when he asks Robert, "Have you ever had the feeling while you were fucking that you were really together with her? I've never felt anything but loneliness when I was in a woman," one understands that it is impossible for him to be *together* with anyone because he is so frightened.

A second reaction to the absence of women is the formation of a homo-erotic bond between the two men. After Bruno "rescues" Robert and the two drive off in his truck, he puts on the record "The More I See You, The More I Want You" and regards Robert affectionately as the latter snuggles down under his blanket to get warm. At first their friendship is tentative; when Robert imposes the intimacy of spontaneously enacting the pantomime for the school children on Bruno, the noose appears again, this time at the end of a rope that swings between them as they sit laughing and panting at the end of their show. Later Bruno tells Robert that he felt helpless and furious. In a parody of marriage, Robert, hurt, takes his blankets and announces that he won't sleep in the cab anymore. Later, the friendship consolidated, Robert persuades Bruno to sneak away from a projecting job he has volunteered for, and the two leave for an evening of high jinx. The next morning finds them both sleeping in the cab again. The erotic tension in their last scene together, which erupts into momentary fisticuffs, is sufficiently blatant for Wenders to comment, "We called that . . . the Love Scene."[22]

The third reaction is primarily Robert's. Having failed to live successfully with a woman—"I'm not *me* when I'm with her," he insists that one must learn how. Always the initiator, he sets off alone the morning after the "Love Scene" and takes the train. Unlike Wilhelm in *Wrong Move,* the men in *Kings* do not leave each other at the end to escape, but to go back to the world they had tried to escape—the world of women.

When asked why male–female relationships never work out in his films, Wenders replied:

> I know maybe a dozen men quite well, friends or people I see often. Of these twelve, not one . . . knows how he should live with his wife, that is, knew, because in the meantime he's given up. . . . The possible exceptions . . . were simply the ones that repressed the most.[23]

To live with a woman and retain one's own identity—the quest goes on, for no Wenders hero to date has solved that problem. The happily married hero of *American Friend* turns out to be one of those "that repressed the most."

A third Wenders theme, familiar from the previous films, is the Americanization of Germany. American icons—Wilhelm's varsity jacket, Bruno's overalls, Robert's hula hoop, Coca-Cola signs, and American music—abound as usual. When Bruno tells Robert that in the midst of fighting with a former girlfriend, a rock and roll tune with words appropriate to the situation popped into his head, Robert replies, "The Yanks have colonized our subconscious." Sitting in the abandoned American patrol hut, enjoying the rugged, careless, male ambiance of its departed inhabitants, Robert calls their casual absorption of the appealing foreign culture to account. Who and what are they besides products of this culture?

Titled *In the Course of Time* in German, *Kings* addresses this question by having each man go back in time, as it were, to confront his past: Robert to his father's newspaper office, Bruno to the Rhine island. Only by confronting his past, Wenders believes, can a person free himself sufficiently from the trammels of the present to be able to face the future capable of change, which is to say, creatively.

The Rhine figures prominently in all three trilogy films. Asked why, Wenders replied that because he had grown up near the Rhine, he wanted to film there as kind of research into his own past similar to that undertaken by the characters in *Kings*.²⁴ (The view from the hills in *Wrong Move* overlooks the Rhine town of Boppard, Wenders' mother's hometown.)

Both *Wrong Move* and *Kings* delve even further into the past, tracing remnants from the Nazi era that have survived into the present. *Wrong Move* does so at greater length. Soon after meeting Laertes, Wilhelm identifies him as an "old Nazi." Learning that he participated in the 1936 Olympics, Wilhelm asks him if he, like Hitler, refused to shake Jesse Owens' hand. Laertes replies that he didn't make the finals and thus never had the opportunity. "But in those days," he says, "I probably wouldn't have shaken a black man's hand." "And now?" Wilhelm asks, but Laertes is silent.²⁵ Loyalties from his past remain strong: on the train to Bonn the conductor salutes Laertes. Later he explains to Wilhelm that the conductor was his adjutant when he commanded the concentration camp at Wilna.

Laertes lives as a vagabond, probably to avoid being captured and tried as a war criminal, and he does penance at night, flagellating himself and sleeping on the floor. His penance, however, is without repentance. "I saved a lot of Jews if they were professionals," he tells Wilhelm after singing a cynical ballad about one that he had killed. "It's all the same to me," he chants in the song's refrain. When the group finds the industrialist's dead body, Laertes responds by playing his harmonica.

Wilhelm's reaction to Laertes is hardly more enlightened. Wilhelm hates the old man blindly and tries to kill him. He won't listen when Laertes, shaken out of his cynicism, tries to explain: "The times were completely different then, you must understand that! We drew a line, almost like you now, between the political and the natural . . . , and in the end came the most awful politics." Only later does Wilhelm acknowledge that he should have tried to learn from the old man. Mignon, too, has little desire to hear about the past; when Laertes begins to talk about the 1936 Olympics, she covers her ears.

Wilhelm's dream expresses his resentment in particularly gruesome terms. He tells Laertes:

> I dreamed that you would die. A few hours before you awaited death, you would commit yourself, carefully, to a mausoleum under the main road. Until death overtook you, a child would keep you company. The child would stand next to you, and the mausoleum would be closed with a giant stone. I dreamed the whole time of the total darkness in which the child next to you had to stand until you died. It was my child.

Wilhelm feels the older generation has plunged his into darkness but neglects to find a constructive way out of this darkness, waiting instead for the older generation to die. "The water used to be clean and pure here," Wilhelm tells Laertes on the ferry, where he hopes to speed up the process of skimming off the older generation by killing the old man. He feels the past is poisoning his life but eventually acknowledges that the past can't be annihilated.

Writing in 1961 Hans Habe complained, "The generation that is between 18 and 30 today licks self-pityingly at the wounds that we have suffered. Not once are their complexes and traumas their own: they're ours."[26] Habe further faults the smug self-righteousness of this generation for blocking any real political initiative. He had early drawn the profile that Handke and Wenders would fill out with Wilhelm, who remarks that everything political is alien to him. "I couldn't formulate my needs in political terms." Wenders notes that his heroes' excursions into Germany's past are personal rather than political. "Lazy politics. They're not at all interested in it as political history; they're interested in it as individualists."[27]

In *Kings* the heroes also venture into Germany's past, but here the old Nazis are less symbolic, more real. The first is the old cinema owner that Bruno interviews in the film's prologue.

> OWNER: . . . after 1951, you see I wasn't allowed to run it [his theater] for years, because of the Third Reich and all that, you know—that's just the way it was.
> BRUNO: Why couldn't you run it?
> OWNER: Well, because I was a member of the party, you know, the SPD, no, eh, the NSPDAD [*sic*] or whatever it was called, you know, *that* party. And I was in court from 1950–51 to get my theater back; that happened to a lot of people with theaters back in those days.

Bruno merely smirks. When he meets Pauline at the midway, she is carrying a Hitler-head candle (which actress Lisa Kreuzer had found for sale at a gas station near the border!).[28] The two joke about it—"Feuer von dem Führer" (fire from the Führer [Hitler]), Bruno remarks as he lights his cigarette. Their scene together is cut between scenes of Robert confronting his father. Thus Nazism is cinematically portrayed as dividing the generations. Although Robert doesn't accuse his father of Nazism, he does accuse him of tyrannizing the family, a custom associated with the older generation in Germany, whose Prussian heritage was claimed by the Nazis. Like the cinema owner, Robert's father as a newspaperman could hardly have kept his job without joining the Party. More, therefore, may lie behind Robert's resentment of his father than he actually states. (When Tom Farrell asked Wenders if his father had been a Nazi, Wenders replied, "My father was a fascist, but I love him,"[29] a remark which strengthens my conviction that we are meant to read between the lines here and see Robert's father as an old Nazi.) Yet Bruno and Robert are not as self-righteous as Wilhelm. Rather than reject the past, they learn from and/or try to teach the older generation.

Fritz Lang, to whom *Kings* refers three times, is a shadowy pivotal presense connecting many of the film's themes. In the prologue the cinema owner mentions that Lang's *Niebelungen* had the longest piano score, thus recalling both the glory days of German cinema, whose downfall was precipitated by the Nazis. Two photographs of Lang appear in the film. After Bruno inspects the suicide's wrecked car, Robert picks up a photograph from Godard's *Contempt* and cuts out Lang's head. At the end of the film a picture of Lang hangs on the wall behind the female cinema owner, who has closed her theater. Figuratively he is the father who taught her that "film is the art of seeing." Figuratively, too, Bruno's lost father is

Kings of the Road (1976)
Bruno lights his cigarette from the Hitler-head candle held by Pauline (Lisa Kreuzer).
(*Courtesy Gray City, Inc.*)

Wenders' lost film father: Lang. Significantly Lang's picture appears both times in the context of tragedy or loss. Forced by Nazism to leave Germany, Lang had to adapt his art and life to a foreign culture. He was the original Americanized German. When he tried to work in Germany's altered industry in the 1950s, he found it wasn't easy to go home again. "The truth is," Wenders wrote in an obituary for Lang, "Lang was treated very badly in Germany."[30]

If Lang and other emigrés of the 30s went to America to escape Nazism, German youngsters of Wenders' generation embraced American culture as a way of escaping the taint of Nazism, which, for many, clung to everything German. When Jan Dawson asked Wenders if it wasn't unusual for a people to make folk heroes out of an occupying army, he replied, "Yes, but that's what happened here. They weren't disliked at all. They were accepted because of the guilt feeling and the need to cover that hole. We covered it with chewing gum."[31]

As noted in the previous chapter, however, postwar Germans followed an age-old precedent in looking to America for all that was lacking in German society. Goethe was an ardent Americanophile, who at one point considered emigrating to America. His Lothario shares this enthusiasm. Having served under Lafayette during the American Revolution, Lothario is determined to create a utopian society on his own estate. "Here or nowhere is America!" he cries. There is double irony in the implicit comparison between Therese's soulless suburb of Frankfurt in *Wrong Move* and Lothario's utopian experiment for anyone who remembers the line from Goethe, for Frankfurt is considered Germany's most "American" city. Wenders' films stand somewhere on the edge of Germany's American Dream, drawing deeply on an ambivalence both present and past. That ambivalence would become even more wrenching in *The American Friend.*

6

The American Friend

A long-time admirer of Patricia Highsmith, Wenders acquired the rights to her *Ripley's Game* before it was published and in the fall of 1976 went into production with it, using the working title "Rule without Exception." The title changed several more times and eventually became *The American Friend (Der amerikanische Freund,* 1977). Lead actor Bruno Ganz recalls that after the first rushes Wenders said, "That's exactly the way I've been working up to now and that's exactly how I don't want to go on working."[1] It is not clear what Wenders saw in those early rushes that he wanted to change, but *American Friend* emerged as a film that both looked and felt different from Wenders' earlier productions. "If any of the young German filmmakers can manage to break out of that circle of initiates and address a wider public without giving up his own signature, then it is Wim Wenders," wrote one German critic about the film.[2] Wenders was perceived as leading the way toward popularizing the New German Cinema, though arguably the Schlöndorff/von Trotta production of *The Lost Honor of Katharina Blum (Die verlorene Ehre der Katharina Blum,* 1975) and Herzog's *Stroszek* (1977) should share the credit. (Schlöndorff's *Tin Drum* and Fassbinder's *Marriage of Maria Braun* were still a year off.) Certainly *American Friend*'s suspense–thriller subject matter, the large budget, and the internationally known stars (Bruno Ganz and Dennis Hopper) were aimed at winning a larger audience.

Yet much continued as before. Wenders' thematic preoccupations (travel, Americanization, male friendship) were written large across the production. "I thought I had room enough for my own stories inside the structure of the novel," he said.[3] Martin Müller suggests that a large budget had little effect on Wenders' working methods: "We still shot right up until all the money was gone and then, in the middle of the Paris shoot, we had to stop and find more."[4] Bruno Ganz describes Wenders' already familiar openness to *trouvailles.*

> What really fascinates me about Wim is the unbelievable alertness with which he responds to reality. If, for example, a house with scaffolding shows up somewhere in the surroundings, then he is guaranteed to find a way to integrate it into the film.[5]

Wenders' attraction to Highsmith's work was in some respects an extension of his collaboration with Handke, who admired the exactness of her prose.[6] Handke was reading several of her novels at the time he wrote *The Goalie's Anxiety*, and the preciseness with which Highsmith describes her characters' feelings, particularly their reactions to place, undoubtedly influenced the *Goalie*. Friends with Highsmith, Handke took Wenders to meet her in 1974.

Numerous film adaptations of Highsmith have appeared through the years, most notably Alfred Hitchcock's *Strangers on a Train* (1951). In the same year that *American Friend* was released, Hans W. Geissendörfer made *The Glass Cell* (*Der gläserne Zelle,* 1977) from Highsmith's 1964 novel by the same name. Unlike other adaptors of Highsmith, however, Wenders concentrated neither on the amorality of the hero nor the innocence of his victim, but on the chemistry between them. And as he did when filming Handke, Wenders captured the essence of her prose in images that were "ever so precise."[7]

Jonathan Zimmermann (Bruno Ganz), a framemaker of slender means, lives in an old apartment block near Hamburg's waterfront with his wife Marianne (Lisa Kreuzer) and their son. Jonathan suffers from a blood disease that could claim his life at any time. An old-world craftsman of pure values, he refuses to shake the hand of Tom Ripley (Dennis Hopper), a expatriated American art dealer of shady reputation. Ripley deals in paintings from an American artist named Derwatt, who pretends to be dead so that his paintings will bring higher prices. Ripley, a neurotic, dresses like a cowboy, talks to himself on a cassette recorder, and lives alone in a huge dilapidated mansion filled with "American Pop" artifacts: a jukebox, a Coca-Cola machine, a flourescent Canada Dry sign hanging over a pool table. Ripley strikes one as vaguely homosexual—he manifests no interest in women, knows only men, hugs and kisses Derwatt by way of greeting him.

Ripley is evidently attracted to Jonathan when they first meet, for Jonathan's snub wounds him deeply. When a gangster friend of his, Raoul Minot (Gerard Blain), asks for a man with a clean record to murder rival gangsters for him, Ripley suggests Jonathan, then regrets his rashness. In an attempt to make amends he visits Jonathan and offers friendship; this time Jonathan is more fascinated than repelled by Ripley and his gauche Americanisms. But Ripley is too late to head off Jonathan's corruption at the hands of Minot, who woos him with fear (that his disease is getting worse), money, and the promise of a specialist's diagnosis. Jonathan commits two murders, the first in the tunnels of the Paris Metro, the second, aided by Ripley, on a Trans-European-Express train travelling between Munich and Hamburg.

Meanwhile Jonathan's marriage, which initially appears warm and supportive if not passionate, begins to disintegrate. His wife Marianne grows suspicious of what she senses are his shady dealings; moreover, she feels abandoned and sees Ripley as her competitor, as indeed he is. Wenders at no time suggests a homosexual liaison between Jonathan and Ripley, but the relationship is clearly homoerotic, based on an attraction of opposites, shared enthusiasms, and lust for adventure.

The American Friend (1977)
Jonathan (Bruno Ganz) reassures Marianne (Lisa Kreuzer).
(Courtesy Road Movies)

Eventually one group of gangsters discovers the Jonathan–Ripley–Minot connection and prepares a nighttime attack on Ripley's mansion. Jonathan helps defend it, and he and Ripley vanquish the gangsters, who arrive in a stolen ambulance. Marianne appears and offers Jonathan a reconciliation, but Ripley advises her that he and Jonathan have work to do first. She agrees to drive for her exhausted husband while Ripley drives the ambulance full of bodies. They arrive on a lonely beach, where sand, sea, and sky are pearl-colored in the early morning light. Ripley sets fire to the ambulance, whose orange explosion contrasts expressively with the white background. It climaxes Jonathan's adventure with Ripley. He pushes Marianne back into their car and drives off across the beach without Ripley. He intends to resume his family life, but exhausted and euphoric he drives off the road, blacks out, and dies as the car heads toward the ocean. Just before it reaches the sea, Marianne pulls on the hand brake. She gets out and looks glumly at Ripley sitting on an old pier post and singing to himself. Sitting beside New York's Westside Highway, Derwatt stands up suddenly and walks off. The male bond continues even in death.

The male buddy mystique of *Kings* is heightened in *American Friend* and its sexual overtones intensified. Borrowing from the conventions of romantic comedy, Ripley and Jonathan become friends only after a period of intense dislike (cf. Peter and Ellie in *It Happened One Night*). To cement their friendship they exchange gifts, small optical toys, one of which shows nude females posing in various lighting set-ups. Ironically Ripley and Jonathan rally round this male in-joke, but neither evinces as much interest in women as in one another. When Marianne arrives at the end of this particular scene, Jonathan stares shame-faced at the floor and Ripley leaves quickly. Marianne is jealous, and all three act as though Jonathan had been caught having an affair. Ripley embraces Jonathan each time they successfully dispatch their victims, and after the train murder Jonathan goes to the back of the train, leans out the window and screams with joy and relief, a metaphorical orgasm.

At times the two men unconsciously synchronize their gestures. Angered at himself for committing the first murder, Jonathan smashes a picture frame. Moments later Ripley walks into the workshop and picks up a small piece of the frame that has fallen to the floor. He draws the piece of frame across his forehead over a spot corresponding to one where Jonathan has a bandaid on *his* forehead and asks Jonathan about the wound. Then he lays the piece on the counter where Jonathan picks it up and runs it over his bandage. Later, locked in the train toilet with a corpse, Jonathan, on a hint from Ripley, finds a ticket in the dead man's pocket and slides it under the door for the anxious conductor. As the ticket appears, Ripley, outside the door, smiles with relief, and inside the toilet Jonathan repeats the grin.

In one scene Ripley acknowledges the limitations of male friendship, much as Robert does in *Kings*. ''I want to be your friend,'' he tells Jonathan, ''but friendship isn't possible.'' Yet over them, in the tavern where they sit, an ad for beer reads ''*echt*'' (genuine).

Marianne is part of the home and security that Jonathan gives up in joining the gangsters. When Jonathan sits alone by the ringing telephone, knowing Minot is calling, he twists the wedding band on his finger, unconsciously indicating the price of his compliance. He is a gentle husband and father, but there is no magnetism between husband and wife. (The familiar ambivalence towards women and sex is betrayed in one humorous scene in which Jonathan comes into his doctor's office, begins to rest his arm in the stirrup at the end of the examination table, does a double take, and finally sits on the table resting both arms in the stirrups.) Lisa Kreuzer, who played Marianne, complained that Jonathan supposedly murders in order to leave money for his wife and child but that the relationship as played lends little credence to this rationale. "It was in the book, and it was in the script, but it wasn't in the film."[8] Indeed Jonathan's horrified fascination with nihilistic male behavior becomes a much stronger motivation. "To me," wrote Kreuzer, "Marianne is the victim. . . . A woman without a story."[9] Marianne is left without a story because, to a large extent, Wenders' men are still in that prepubescent frame of mind in which boys don't play with girls and sex is confined to giggling at nude photographs.

In *American Friend* the little-boy games of *Kings'* Bruno and Robert become deadly without ever becoming more grown-up. Vulnerable and irresponsible, Ripley and Jonathan are seduced by violence, but it lends them neither power nor adulthood. To underscore this point Wenders cleverly reinvents the gun as phallus motif. Jonathan stalks his first victim through the Metro tunnels with his supposedly hidden revolver peeking out from under his coat. Noticing his slip, he hastily pulls his coat around him like a man discovering.his fly unzipped. Before the train murders, Jonathan examines his gun in the toilet but forgets to lock the door. When one of the Mafiosi starts to walk in on him, he quickly slams the door like a man caught playing with himself. Clearly the gun is a phallic symbol but in the sense of shame, vulnerability, and exposure rather than potency. By subverting the gun as phallus motif, Wenders illustrates the irrelevance to modern males of the primitive equation of sex and violence with potency, initiation, and adulthood. Despite the atavistic attraction it holds for Jonathan and Ripley, violence in *American Friend* never transcends the level of a child's deadly plaything.

American Friend takes place in four major metropolitan areas: Hamburg, Paris, New York, and Munich. Through editing Wenders deliberately confuses the cities. Wenders cuts from Jonathan in Paris to Ripley in New York, and from Ripley on a Hamburg-bound plane to Jonathan on a Hamburg-bound train to a dawn shot of Jonathan walking across the Hamburg waterfront. Sequences in both Hamburg and New York take place in waterfront locations. In Paris Wenders chose to use a section called "little Manhattan," where a small replica of the Statue of Liberty stands in the Seine. One interurban sequence is cut as follows:

—pan of the Paris cityscape over "Little Manhattan," shot from Jonathan's hotel room.
—shot of the phone ringing in Jonathan's Hamburg apartment.
—real Manhattan skyline (from Brooklyn).
—sequence in Derwatt's loft (Manhattan).

—Jonathan's Paris hotel room; his telephong rings.
—Minot talking on the telephone from his balcony in Paris.
—second pan of the Paris cityscape from Jonathan's hotel in which the tiny figure of Minot appears waving from his balcony.
—Jonathan hanging up the telephone.
—close-up of an elevator counter (Jonathan's hotel).
—close-up of the faked medical report in Jonathan's hands followed by a sequence in Minot's apartment. As Jonathan closes the report the Statue of Liberty in the Seine becomes visible.

The sequence gives the impression that all cities are one and hints broadly that their unity follows an American model.

Camera placement causes the Statue of Liberty to replace the faked medical report in Jonathan's hands and links his betrayal with America (as was the goalie's since American coins led the police to him). Minot has faked the report, but Ripley, the American, has set Jonathan up in the first place. The liberty he offers Jonathan in the form of male friendship and an escape from domesticity comes only at a price.

Wenders describes *American Friend* as a film "full of love and full of hatred [for the 'American Friend'] but . . . not . . . a film that has found a way out of this antagonism."[10] Wenders sets up lines of battle in the film that are familiar from German literary and political traditions. Ripley, the American entrepreneur, is contrasted to Jonathan, the European craftsman. Jonathan's surname, Zimmermann—meaning "carpenter"—both suggests his profession as a picture framer and stresses his status as a craftsman. "I make money," says Ripley deprecatingly of himself; that he makes it dishonestly is merely an extension of this fact. He admires and envies Jonathan's craftsmanship, for he is the clichéd American, lacking tradition and culture, overly friendly, and concerned with money to the point of corruption.

Jonathan is eventually corrupted by money. In one sequence he sits in his workshop and picks up a sheet of gold leaf with a pair of tweezers; he lets the leaf float into his hand and blows on it until it clings as it might to the hand of a statue; then he goes to the telephone to call Minot and picks up the receiver with his gold-leafed palm. The lure of money has won out.

Jonathan's association with Ripley is vaguely shameful, not simply because Ripley is a shady character, but because he is an American. During a fight with Jonathan, Marianne accuses him of neglecting her and lying to her; Jonathan tries to reassure her, but when she throws out the words, "you and your *American* friend," he slaps her.

The artist versus the entrepreneur or philistine and the association of the philistine with Americans has a long tradition in German literature. Fritz Stern writes,

> From the 1870's on, conservative writers in imperial Germany expressed the fear that the German soul would be destroyed by "Americanization." . . . The artist was thought to personify the human condition . . . and no theme is more characteristic . . . than the struggle between the artist and the philistine.[11]

Links to anti-Semitism were inevitable. In 1891 Julius Langbehn wrote: "The crude cult of money, a North-American and at the same time a Jewish characteristic, predominates in Berlin more and more."[12]

In *American Friend* German prewar political theories are suggested by the "international conspiracy" that begins with Derwatt in New York, whose forgeries bring Jonathan into contact with Ripley in Hamburg, who sets him up for Minot in Paris. Contrary to the gangsters in Highsmith's book, who are German and Italian, the gangsters in *American Friend* are French, American, and Jewish–American. Thus Jonathan's "enemies" are those of Germany from 1870 through the Third Reich.

In Wenders' film the traditional myths are altered only slightly, but enough to skew their prewar meaning. Jonathan, the artisan, is, like Wenders' other heroes, already partially Americanized when the film begins: he loves rock music and chewing gum. Far from being a man with no culture, Ripley possesses a rich and vibrant culture which Wenders enthusiastically shows us in Ripley's dress (blue jeans, cowboy boots, and cowboy hat) and furnishings (a jukebox, Coca-Cola machine, pool table, and neon Canada Dry sign). Just as Jonathan has already adopted some of this culture, so he colludes with the American and the Frenchman in a venture which both liberates and destroys him. Finally the Jew, his first target, is an arbitrary enemy who becomes his victim. Thus Wenders reinterprets the myths from a postwar perspective.

If Wenders' love and hate for America is more sharply etched in *American Friend* than it had been previously, his view of cinema is more polarized. The film alludes to only two types of cinema: early cinema and pornographic cinema. Cinema in its infancy is connected to Jonathan's son Daniel, who in various scenes plays with a zoetrope and a large wooden model of a Maltese cross (the invention that made cinema possible) and keeps a moving-light picture of a steam locomotive named "The General" (presumably named after Buster Keaton's) by his bed. Early cinema is innocent cinema and is associated with the child. At the other extreme are the American gangsters who make pornographic films and visit Europe in order to work out an agreement for an international co-production. Portrayed on the one hand as an innocent, Jonathan too is associated with early cinema. He owns the zoetrope and the model of the Maltese cross and stands by Daniel's bed when we see the moving-light picture. Yet his innocence is compromised: he trafficks with the gangsters, eventually receiving a kiss from the gangsters' lead actress Mona. When Ripley tells him that Jonathan detected a change in the blue of the forged Derwatt, the artist credits him with having a better eye than Ripley. "Not for long," Ripley replies, ostensibly meaning that Jonathan will die from his disease, but also, perhaps, that he will be corrupted since innocence and vision are related for Wenders. While he was making *American Friend* Wenders told an interviewer that film as an art form had developed so far that one couldn't take it any farther innocently.[13] Thus Jonathan's inability to remain innocent parallels Wenders' view of cinema as unable to remain in its early stages.

The American Friend (1977)
Boy play: Ripley (Dennis Hopper) and Jonathan (Bruno Ganz).
(*Courtesy Road Movies*)

Asked about the gangsters in *American Friend,* Wenders replied, "I had so much trouble with this whole gangster idea. . . . I mean these are impossible gangsters. I just couldn't take it seriously, and I thought it was okay not to take it seriously."[14] Indeed Wenders' gangster–thriller jumps in and out of its genre mode, frequently invoking the genre's language only to undercut it. Wenders had already established a pattern of undercutting genre situations in his previous films. *Goalie*, an anti-thriller, frequently set up suspenseful situations, such as Bloch crossing paths with unsuspecting policemen, which never led to anything. Oddly enough *Alice* often refers to the suspense genre but never fulfills the expectations engendered by its genre set-ups because it isn't a suspense film. For example, Lisa sneaks away from Philip's bedside, leaving him a note. Philip pretends to sleep, but as soon as she has left, he watches her through the venetian blinds as she gets into a taxi in the street below. Later, looking through the binoculars on top of the Empire State Building, he catches a glimpse of her leaving the hotel again in a taxi and realizes she will not be meeting him as promised. For so much intrigue and spying to result in a straightforward plea for Philip to take Alice to Amsterdam disappoints one's expectations. When Philip stops in front of his hotel in Wuppertal after having left Alice with the police, a shot of him inside the car reveals the side door opening and someone's shadow falling across his seat. The suspense is relieved when Alice slides into the seat, and audiences usually laugh, acknowledging that they have been tricked, their expectations undercut.

In *American Friend* Wenders occasionally breaks unabashedly into crime genre film language. When, during the train escapade, Jonathan finds he has too much to handle, Ripley comes leaping out of nowhere like a latter-day Errol Flynn to save him. With slick, perfectly timed teamwork, they knock out a second gangster who comes looking for the first. Likewise the final confrontation with gangsters plays straight until its final moments. Jonathan and Ripley run across the street; a passing car squeals its brakes to avoid hitting Ripley and alerts the Mafia boss (Sam Fuller), who waits in the ambulance across the street and blows smoke from his cigar. In the fight which follows, Fuller rolls down a flight of steps leading to the beach in a canted shot reminiscent of Fuller's own films. Finally Mona, the Mafia moll, gets out of the ambulance, surveys the carnage, picks up her purse, and flounces off petulantly into the night, bringing laughs from an audience used to seeing females in Mona's position thrown on the mercy of the victors.

Elsewhere in *American Friend* Wenders sets up crime genre situations that turn out to be meaningless, much as he does in *Alice* and *Goalie*. Toward the beginning Jonathan opens a safe so secretively that he looks like a safecracker, but it is his own safe! Later Ripley apprehends a mysterious trespasser breaking into his house, only to find that it is his old friend Minot. Well-known from the film's publicity posters is a shot of Ripley driving his car and holding what appears to be a walkie-talkie to his ear, looking like a Texas Ranger. The "walkie-talkie," however, is a tape-recorder into which the neurotic Ripley talks to himself. In this scene he replays the previous day's introspection. In another sequence Jonathan returns from

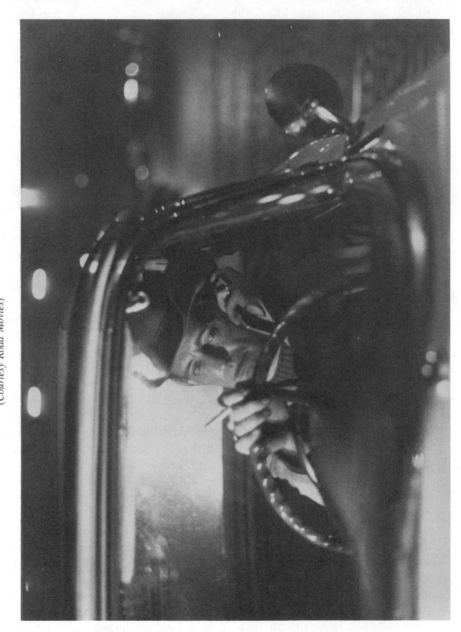

The American Friend (1977)
Ripley listening to his cassette recorder.
(*Courtesy Road Movies*)

Paris in the early morning to find his house empty. Normally a return to an unex-pectedly empty house is a prelude to some kind of attack in a gangster film. We think that perhaps the gangsters have kidnapped the family. Instead Marianne and Daniel are hiding to surprise him.[15]

Wenders toys with genre conventions but doesn't simply deconstruct the genre; he also invents new images for it. For example, an extreme long shot of Ripley walking along the West Side Highway from an office building where one gangster sits swinging an orange scarf shows Ripley's tiny figure through an orange swirl from which the camera moves back to reveal the gangster sitting in the win-dow. The shot illustrates Ripley's conversation with Derwatt moments before: "I'm confused," he tells Derwatt. "A little older, a little more confused . . . " the painter replies. "If you close the door, they'll come through the windows." The shot with the orange scarf seems to imply Ripley becoming ever more en-tangled in the gangsters' affairs just as Derwatt's words, taken in a literal sense, imply the impossibility of keeping them out.

American Friend went through numerous title changes, one of which was "The Broken Frame" (*Der kaputte Rahmen*), referring to the framing of Jonathan. Wenders dropped the title but kept the idea of inventing images and sequences around the idea of framing Jonathan. Jonathan's profession, of course, lends itself to such imagery: in an early scene he holds up a frame and looks through it as he prepares to frame Derwatt's painting. When he receives the faked telegram, he paces nervously around the shop and bumps his head on a row of frames hanging on a rack. Later, Ripley comes in and requests to see a frame he has ordered from Jonathan. He stands in the back of Jonathan's shop holding half the frame—his half of the frame-up. When Jonathan gives Ripley his finished picture, Ripley lays down the picture and repeats "Framed!"

As a thriller, *American Friend* is more meditative than suspenseful, but Wenders often creates tension by purely formal means, through sound and color. The film's music consists of several dissonant chords which convey a sense of im-minent danger and a high level of irritation, thus creating tension when the story does not.

At times animal sounds heighten the tension and correlate with Jonathan's darker moods. In one scene he walks out on the small balcony of his son's bedroom and waves good-by to Daniel and Marianne. Watching them leave, his thoughts turn inwards; he becomes agitated and frightened because of the faked telegram he received the day before. The cries of gulls circling above him suddenly become very loud and raucous on the sound-track; he turns and stumbles back into the bedroom, tripping over Daniel's toy cable car while an inner monologue begins. In the background the machines in the harbor make a loud thumping sound, like the thumping of Jonathan's heart. The scene in which Jonathan breaks the frame in his workshop is intercut with shots of Ripley coming along the alley to visit him. In the alley, dogs are barking angrily; the sound of Jonathan smashing the frame overlaps with that of the barking dogs.

(Wenders experimented with a sound system for *American Friend* which had been pioneered by Robert Altman in *Nashville*. It consisted of three stereo recorders coordinated by a directional microphone, which allow one to record sound over a much larger area without one sound drowning out another.)

Like the music, the color in *American Friend* shocks and irritates. When Jonathan comes out of the Metro after shooting his first victim, the city is bathed in a lurid red–orange. As he leaves Paris later, the sky is purple. Hamburg's harbor glows orange at times and purple at others. To achieve these garish effects Wenders and Müller, using the then-new Eastman Color Negative II, left filters off their lenses, did not correct for neon lights, and mixed artificial with natural light.

The intense color illustrates the clash between Jonathan's quiet life and the gangsters' world. Jonathan's apartment and workshop are dark and natural in tone, decorated and lit to achieve a "Rembrandt brown."[16] By contrast red and orange are associated with the gangsters. Jonathan's hotel room in Paris is decorated in red and orange and orange construction cranes appear threateningly outside his window. Ripley's bedroom vibrates with red, which is used in the satin sheets and curtains. The connection between red and blood is illustrated most dramatically when the Sam Fuller character falls to his death on the steps near the harbor, his blood lit by red lights near the waterfront.

Green is also associated with Ripley. The pool table, where we find him once eating breakfast and once taking Polaroid pictures of himself, is green and is lit from above by a Canada Dry sign, which casts a green glow. Later when he talks to Jonathan on the telephone, he is bathed in a green light. The color we often associate with illness and "little men from Mars" emphasizes Ripley's weirdness.

American Friend's formal system is much more sophisticated than that of Wenders' previous films. In addition to the sound and color systems, elliptical cutting, and play with genre motifs, Wenders weaves a network of repetition and variation through *American Friend* that is far more intricate than the parallelism of earlier films. For example, the break-up of Jonathan's family life is worked out through repetitions. When Jonathan tries calling Marianne from Paris, we see the telephone ringing in the empty apartment. She happens to be out. When he arrives home from Paris, the apartment appears to be empty: Marianne and Daniel are hiding and jump out to surprise him. When he returns after quarrelling with Marianne in his shop, the apartment is empty again; she has left him.

Throughout the film shots of Jonathan with his chest thrust out and his head thrown back recur frequently. He takes this posture while having his sternum punctured for blood marrow samples, and it suggests him as a kind of sacrificial victim. Upright he takes this posture when he talks to Ripley on the telephone and in the train toilet when he puts the garotte around his own neck and pulls the cord tight. Wenders also shows him upright in this position walking or running through a variety of tunnels or tunnel-like spaces: the Elbe Tunnel in Hamburg, the Metro tunnels in Paris, the aisles of the art dealer's storeroom, and the tomblike cement trenches around Ripley's house. The tunnel shots suggest the victim in a maze.

Other shots of Jonathân running also suggest a man in a maze. When he receives the faked telegram, he runs, in an extreme high shot, across the waterfront from his shop to a subway station, down a complex of blue escalators and through the Elbe Tunnel to his doctor's office. Another time he runs down a flight of stairs and through the same tunnel to meet his doctor at the other end. Later he negotiates a complex of silver escalators at Orly, and still later runs down the up-escalator in the Paris Metro after killing his first victim. Toward the end of the film he runs, again in extreme high shot, across the waterfront from his workshop to his apartment.

The end of *American Friend* contrasts strikingly with the rest of the film. The cities fade away, the colors are muted, and driving dominates for the first time in this film. The maze, like the circle in *Kings,* has been broken. Rolling across the beach at dawn the ambulance blends into the white background: sand, surf, sky. Only Jonathan's orange Volkswagen stands out against the landscape, whose uniform color creates an aura of other-worldliness. The exploding ambulance gives Jonathan's adventure an apocalyptic end from which he believes he can simply drive away. Instead he drives over the sea wall and dies by the sea. "It's getting so dark," he complains to Marianne, and one recalls the man in *Alabama* who dies while driving, the light getting dimmer and dimmer. The sound of waves lapping on the beach carries into the next scene in which Derwatt is sitting by the West Side Highway. The sound connects the dead Jonathan with the "dead" Derwatt, whose decisive movement at that moment suggests a determination to return to life.

The mysticism pervading the last scene recalls German Romanticism, a tradition Wenders had already invoked by using the *Bildungsroman* as the basis of *Wrong Move, Alice,* and *Kings.* Other references to the sea, with their implications of longing, travel, and death, link *American Friend* to Romanticism. These references primarily involve Jonathan. Even as a contented bourgeois, he looks into his stereopticon at a beach scene with boats, an indication perhaps of an as-yet-unspecified longing to escape. When he waves good-by to his family from the balcony of his apartment, the camera pans across the ships in the harbor. The print Ripley brings Jonathan to frame pictures ships in a harbor and is captioned *"Des Auswanderers Sehnsucht"* ("The Emigrant's Longing"). When, no longer far from death, Jonathan comes home and finds Marianne gone, he looks through the Venetian blinds at ships in the harbor and then faints. For Jonathan the escape promised by the sea is always in a picture or outside a window. Appropriately his final escape takes him outside the window to the edge of the sea. One recalls the story Philip tells Alice in which the little boy travels until he reaches the sea where he remembers his mother. Jonathan, too, seems called by a primordial mother when he reaches the sea.

German Romantic painter Caspar David Friedrich, of whom Wenders is "a great admirer,"[17] pictures the sea in connection with death. In his *Stages of Life* (1835, Leipzig) he paints himself as "old age" walking invincibly toward the sea.

Two other works by Friedrich are particularly relevant not only to *American Friend*, but to Wenders' other films. These are a sepia wash entitled *View through a Window* (1806, Vienna) and an oil painting, *Woman at the Window* (1822, Berlin). The sepia wash pictures a window open onto a river with the mast and rigging of a sailboat dominating the view. The oil painting shows essentially the same window with Friedrich's wife looking out of it. According to art historian Lorentz Eitner, the open window pictured by German Romantic painters parallels "the lust for travel or escape which ran through romantic literature."[18] The presence of the sailboat in Friedrich's paintings reinforces Eitner's interpretation. He further notes that although the open window signifies a wanderlust or romantic longing, the window itself provides a threshold or barrier which keeps the outside world safely at a distance, thus the windows and picture frames through which Jonathan looks at ships. Wenders acknowledges that the romanticism in many of his films stems from the characters' "longing for something undefined."[19] Often he poses his characters looking out of windows without speaking. In *Wrong Move* Wilhelm looks out his bedroom window and then puts his fists through the glass. Later we see him asleep, dreaming of ships.

Dying by the sea, Jonathan has passed over the threshold. Wenders would explore the relationship between longing, escape, and death further in his next film *Lightning over Water*.

American Friend was a critical and box office success. Wenders had indeed caught the attention of a wider public without dropping his own signature. His next project was a science fiction film set in Australia. While scouting locations in the Outback, he received a cable asking him to direct Francis Ford Coppola's newest project, a fiction thriller paying homage to mystery writer Dashiell Hammett. *American Friend* thus opened the way for Wenders to fulfill one of his own romantic longings: to work in an American studio. His decision to accept Coppola's offer would alter the direction of his career though not, to Coppola's chagrin, his way of making films.

7

Hollywood: *Hammett,*
Lightning over Water, and *The State of Things*

Wenders has always been quick to acknowledge his debt to the American film. "I saw 30 or 40 Hawks and Ford films before I saw any European movies,"[1] he told an interviewer (in what is surely an exaggeration). He studied the pacing of Anthony Mann's *Man of the West* on an editing table in film school and later adapted one of Mann's sequences in *Goalie*. In the western, a high shot of a moving train cuts to a close-up of the wheels with steam billowing out from them, which is followed by a long shot of the outlaws riding through a stream with the train moving through the landscape in the background. During the bus journey in *Goalie,* Wenders used a similar rhythm and juxtaposition of shots, including the close-up of the wheels and a long shot showing the bus in the foreground and the train moving at an angle to it in the background.

In *Alice* he paid homage to Hitchcock by placing Philip and Alice at a bus stop on a country road near the airport and then panning to a roadsign reading "Northwest." In *Kings* he quoted the scene from Nicolas Ray's *Lusty Men* in which Robert Mitchum returns to the house in which he lived as a boy, crawls underneath it, and pulls a gun and a comic book from a hiding place beneath the floorboards. In *Kings,* Bruno returns to his childhood home, slides open the bottom step of the porch, and pulls out a tin of comics. In *American Friend,* Wenders not only cast Nicholas Ray and Sam Fuller, but imitated the slick, glossy look, the canted angles, and the neurotic tension that pervade their films.

Wenders' references to Hollywood films are not simple homages but indications of whole modes of styling and thinking about his material that he adopted from the American directors. Mann's quiet pace, Fuller's tension, Ray's evocation of homelessness were attitudes he took over in his films much as he took the idea of two men travelling together from films like Ford's *Two Rode Together* or Dennis Hopper's *Easy Rider*. He even tried out Hitchcock's suspense in *Alice* but not very successfully since his suspense set-ups lack sufficient motivation.

He had learned so much from American film that he was inevitably lured by the prospect of working in America.

An American production, shot in Hollywood, inside a studio, with a producer who understands himself as the center of the film. . . . That tradition was such a myth for me, the American cinema had haunted me for so long, that it was an enormous challenge and opportunity when Francis Coppola invited me to come over and make *Hammett* for him.[2]

Wenders was in Australia scouting locations for a science fiction film when one of Coppola's producers, Fred Roos, wired asking him to direct a film about Dashiell Hammett for Coppola. Wenders had only two books with him at the time—Hammett's *Glass Key* and *Red Harvest.* He took this as a sign that he should agree to the project.

Wenders' interest in Hammett, as well as in other American detective fiction writers, went back to his teen years and was another of the enthusiasms he shared with Peter Handke. In his *Chronik der laufenden Ereignisse*, Handke named his two male leads Sam Beaumont and Philip Spade, references to *The Maltese Falcon's* Sam Spade and *The Glass Key's* Ned Beaumont. (The ''Philip'' presumably refers to Raymond Chandler's Philip Marlowe.) During the film, one of the actresses tells Sam Beaumont the dream about the house full of snakes that Janet Henry describes to Ned Beaumont in *The Glass Key.*

The project was Roos' pet. His interest in Hammett also went back many years and his interest in the film project went back two years to 1975 when he had read Joe Gores' novel *Hammett*, in which the historical Dashiell Hammett becomes involved in an intrigue supposedly resembling one of his own novels. (In fact, Gores' story is much more violent and preposterously convoluted than anything Hammett ever wrote.) Roos persuaded Coppola, who never read it, to option the book and Nicholas Roeg to direct the project. It took a year to resolve all the legal questions involved in creating a film with a completely fictitious story built around an historical figure whose immediate family members were still living. Gores was commissioned to write the script and finished it in February of 1977. Roeg liked it as did François Truffaut, who was asked to direct after Roeg pulled out due to time constraints. Truffaut declined because he had just finished shooting a similar script, but while in Europe, Roos saw *The American Friend*, and decided that Wenders would be his next choice as director of *Hammett*. Ross persuaded Coppola and distributor Mike Medavoy to screen Wenders' films. Medavoy thought Wenders too ''European,''[3] but Coppola flew Wenders to San Francisco and signed him on.

Wenders had a nostalgia for Hammett that surpassed that of Gores and Roos. He rented Hammett's former apartment at 891 Post Street and lived there for six months until the cockroaches finally drove him out. He read every Hammett short story he could find and had the Zoetrope staff collect volumes of information on Hammett. Obviously Wenders was driving the schizophrenia inherent in Gores' original story—using a historical character in a drama of pure fiction—even deeper as he concentrated so intensely on the historical Hammett. He wanted an entirely new script, and Gores tried to oblige. But as the story concentrated more and more on Hammett, it lost track of its detective fiction. With his new scripts getting farther and farther away from his original idea, Gores bowed out of the project.

While Roos looked for a new writer, Wenders looked for a lead actor. He had, by this time, met playwright Sam Shepard and suggested Shepard as both actor and scenarist. Shepard was screen-tested, and Wenders thought the test splendid, but the men with the money said no, presumably because Shepard was at that time still unknown as an actor. As a writer Shepard, whose plays take place in purely mental landscapes, might have restored some integrity to the project by turning Hammett into a symbolic, ahistorical figure like Mae West and Marlene Dietrich in *Mad Dog Blues*, but it was not to be. He promised Wenders they would work together another time and exited gracefully.

Thomas Pope was hired to work on the script instead. He and Wenders decided to bring more of *The Maltese Falcon* into their story and planned to have the characters in Hammett's adventure parallel those he created for *Maltese Falcon*. The idea was to suggest that the film's story had inspired Hammett's book—a bizarre, not to say hubristic notion. "We wanted to create a situation," Pope said, "in which Hammett couldn't do anything to right the wrong, a situation with so many personal and political repercussions that his only recourse is to create Sam Spade to redeem himself and save his own soul."[4] A first draft of this script was finished in March and was approved by the producers. Nevertheless Pope set to work on a second draft which was to incorporate some changes suggested by the studio. Eventually this script too was rejected, victim in part to Coppola's idea that they try taping it as a radio show. (Sam Shepard played Hammett in this taped version.) Since much of the film's meaning depended, presumably, on the audience's ability to make *Wizard-of-Oz*-like connections between Hammett's fictional characters and the "real" people of his adventure, the radio show naturally proved too difficult for an audience to follow. Pope left the project, and a third writer, Dennis O'Flaherty, came in. Meanwhile Wenders took time off to make an impromptu film with Nicholas Ray, who was dying of cancer.

When James Dean died in 1955, Nicholas Ray wrote:

> Through a tragic irony, the escape that James Dean found was total and absolute. But he is mourned through the image of Jim Stark [*Rebel without a Cause*], whose escape was the one he really hoped for, constantly searched for—a full, complete realization of self.[5]

Ray was, in fact, describing himself: a rebel whose search for an escape was really a quest for self-realization. A well-established director in the 1950s, Ray left Hollywood in 1958 and settled in Europe, where he began project after project, which he never completed, his rebellion having been largely consumed by alcohol. He returned to the U.S. in 1969 and in the early 70s spent two years teaching filmmaking at Harpur College in upstate New York. Subsequently he moved to New York City, where he taught acting and directing at New York University and the Lee Strasburg Institute. His Soho loft, where he lived with Susan Schwartz, a woman forty years younger than he, was featured in *American Friend*, in which it became Derwatt's studio. Ray first met Wenders in 1976 just prior to the New York location shooting for *American Friend* and helped write the character of Derwatt. In 1978 he was diagnosed as having cancer and underwent surgery three times. Aware that he had little to show for his last years outside his unfinished *We Can't Go Home Again*, an experiment in split screen technique he had begun with his Harpur students, Ray approached several independent filmmakers about the possibility of making one last film. Wenders, who had remained in close contact with Ray since *American Friend*, responded with an initial $50,000.

The idea for the film was vague. At first Ray expected to make a fiction feature but clearly could not summon the energy for such a project. In the end he and Wenders made an expressionist documentary on their friendship. Most of the film, including interchanges between Wenders and Ray, was scripted, although the title, *Lightning over Water*, comes from a film title Ray improvised when he forgot his lines. Tom Farrell, Ray's former student at Harpur, played himself and, as part of his character, videotaped Ray's last days with a camera borrowed from Zoetrope, Coppola's production company. When it came time to edit, Wenders lacked sufficient filmed footage and was forced to use the videotaped material, which added an element of "cinema verité" to the film.

Wenders used some of his former crew on the film, Martin Schäfer, Peter Pryzgodda, and Martin Müller. Pierre Cottrell, who had produced *American Friend*, and Chris Sievernich, a German production manager based in New York, produced the film. Americans filled out the crew, most notably Edward Lachman, the cinematographer. Lachman, who has worked for a number of European directors including Herzog, Fassbinder, Bertolucci, and Godard, had assisted Robbie Müller on the New York sections of *American Friend*.

Work began when the crew followed Ray to Vassar College to record a lecture he was giving at a retrospective of his films. Later they returned to shoot dialogued scenes in the backstage areas. Throughout the filming, Ray was in and out of the hospital and Wenders in and out of Los Angeles, where Dennis O'Flaherty was working on the *Hammett* script. Ray died on June 16, 1979.

The film within the film that Ray and Wenders discuss making involves an ailing painter who sails to China to find a cure for his disease. Ray really believed they would shoot this scene, and to humor him, Chris Sievernich hired a Chinese junk. After Ray's death, the crew held a wake on the junk and filmed it and themselves.

Too depressed by his work on the film to help with the cutting, Wenders left the footage with Peter Przygodda, who worked on it for a year. His version was shown at Cannes, but it disturbed Wenders, who found it obscure and depressing. After Cannes, Wenders spent three months editing the film with Sievernich, paring down the sometimes bizarre sequences and adding more footage of Ray's companion Susan Schwartz. They also added a voice-over narration spoken by Wenders that included passages from Ray's diary. At times they superimposed the diary passages, still in Ray's handwriting, over the filmed images. This version is currently in circulation.

Wim Wenders and Nicholas Ray Going over a Scene for *Lightning over Water* (1980) *(Courtesy Gray City, Inc.)*

The film begins with a yellow taxi pulling up in front of a cast-iron frame building in lower Manhattan to the accompaniment of the same dissonant chords that raised the hair on one's spine in *American Friend*. In fact the shot deliberately copies that which opens *American Friend*, but instead of Dennis Hopper, Wim Wenders gets out of the cab. Wenders follows the same route Hopper took in the previous film and climbs the stairs to Ray's loft. He has come to give the once great director a chance to make a last film, to "bring himself all together before he dies," as Ray puts it later in the film. Wenders and Ray discuss the film: the story, the actors, the title, for which Ray chooses *Lightning over Water*. They decide to begin by filming Ray's upcoming lecture at Vassar, which follows a screening of his 1952 film *The Lusty Men*. After the lecture Wenders looks at a videotape of Ray's speech which Tom Farrell has made. The two men watch Ray's ghostly form on the monitor while the red light from a neon sign outside throbs on and off like a heartbeat.

Later in the film Ray shows his unfinished *We Can't Go Home Again*. During the screening he gets up and, stooped and emaciated, stands watching his image, still strong and vibrant, on the screen. Director and crew are haunted by Ray's suffering. Wenders dreams that Tom Farrell tries to strangle him.

Wenders is called back to Los Angeles, but before he leaves, Ray checks into the hospital. Wenders visits him, a sequence we see thanks to Farrell's video. Wenders leaves for Los Angeles taking Ray's diary of the last two years with him. Words from the diary appear across the screen as Wenders ponders the dying man's wisdom and courage. When Wenders returns, Ray is rehearsing actor Gerry Bamman in Kafka's *Report to the Academy*, a satirical monologue in which an ape tells of his decision to join the human race. Later Wenders' then-wife Ronee Blakley and Ray rehearse a scene Ray has written based loosely on *King Lear*. Starkly symbolic, the sets and costumes are white while a black cat sits beside Ray's bed. Wenders watches them and dreams that he is on the bed. Ray sits beside him and complains. Finally he faces the camera and calls, "Cut!"

The film cuts to its Epilogue, Ray's wake aboard the Chinese junk. On deck a Chinese urn contains Ray's ashes. "Nick's dying was his last directorial assertion," says one crew member. The film ends with a freeze frame: a long helicopter shot of the junk sailing in New York harbor, Manhattan in the background, and over it writing from Ray's diary,

> I looked into my face and what did I see? No granite rock of identity. Faded blue, drawn skin, and wrinkled lips. And sadness. And the wildest urge to recognize and accept the face of my mother.

More than most, *Lightning* is a film created in the cutting room. In the course of shooting, the directors had little idea where they were going with the film largely because Ray was very feeble and could have died at any time. The assembled material resulted less in a documentary than a personal testimony functioning on a principle of shifting levels of reality. One level, in which we see the crew at work, is reflexive, reminding the audience that we are "in the process of making a film," as Ray tells the Vassar audience. The conversations between Wenders and Ray, which were scripted for the most part, form the core of the film. These become reflexive at one point, however, when Wenders misses his line and starts over. In addition to the staged "reality" in and around Ray's loft and the scenes in which he lectures at Vassar and rehearses Gerry Bamman, which are only partly staged, there are the purely fictional sequences, Wenders' dreams and the *King Lear* scene with Ronee Blakley. These fictional scenes draw upon the immediate reality of the situation and the fantasies of those involved, however, and thus portray a subjective "reality."

Tom Farrell's video sequences punctuate the film, which cuts from Farrell taping to the taped sequences themselves, a shift from scripted shots to the purely spontaneous video. The cuts from film to video emphasize the objective versus subjective tension underlying the film, the conflict between an objectively planned and executed shooting schedule and the live, personal drama which no shooting schedule could contain or control. When Wenders visits a cadaverous Ray in the hospital, a scene captured only on video, the film often probes nearest this subjective drama. Yet the bizarre and ghostly video sequences, while in one sense more "real" than the filmed sequences, have an otherwordly quality that evokes the idea of a battle with death.

These varying levels of reality jostle one another throughout the film. One group of shots shifts from Wenders' dream that Farrell is choking him, on 35mm film, to a video shot of the crew looking on, no longer as substantial as they appear on film but seeming to hover like accusing specters. The next shot, on film, is a slick and shiny Manhattan morning street with Wenders and Farrell, entirely friends, on their way to have breakfast. The sequence illustrates the shifting levels in the film as well as the contrasting effect of the video. Wenders' commentary serves to orient the viewer, who nevertheless must constantly readjust his sense of reality. Yet the shifting levels prepare him for the one unstaged reality which ultimately determines the shape and ethos of the film—Ray's death: objectively the most intransigent reality, but subjectively unreal because none of us know what death is like.

Ray never lived to see the junk though he had written scenes for it. A reminder of his last feature, *55 Days in Peking*, the boat appears at intervals throughout the film. Like a funeral barge, it suggests passage to another world. Ribbons of 35mm film stream from its bow and suggest Ray's immortality through his films and through this film. Yet in its wispy frailty, the wind-blown film stock also images the frailty of human life.

There are three major cutaways to the junk within the main body of the film, and each extends our vision of Ray's death and Wenders' conception of it. Before the first cutaway Ray asks Wenders why he came, and Wenders replies that he wanted to talk to Ray. "About what?" asks Ray. "Dying?" An extreme long shot of the junk, which becomes a very fast tracking and zoom shot, follows immediately, visually iterating the sense of zooming in on death or confronting it directly that Ray's words evoke.

The second cutaway occurs during Gerry Bamman's Kafka performance. Stepping under a ladder intended to represent a cage, the ape-turned-human explains, "Freedom was not what I wanted, but a way out . . . out . . . OUT!"—his volume increasing while he shakes the ladder violently. The junk appears in extreme long shot sailing under a bridge. The shot is quiet, no zoom; the bridge intensifies the idea of passage. As the ape stepped into humanhood as a way out, Ray steps into death. Yet the comparison between Ray and the humanized ape, together with the images of boat and bridge, implies that death is not the end, that Ray somehow transcends mortality as the ape transcended apehood.

The third cutaway begins the Epilogue and occurs after Ray has faced the camera and said, "Cut! Once again the junk appears at a point of confrontation. Again the idea of passage is reinforced when the junk, photographed from directly above, an omniscient viewpoint, sails under a bridge. The use of the boat and bridge to suggest eternity and passage is, like aspects of Wenders' other films, reminiscent of Romantic painter Caspar David Friedrich. In Friedrich's "Woman at the Window" (1822), the river outside the window is usually interpreted as death or the transition out of mortal life, as in the mythical River Styx; the other side of the river toward which the woman looks is said to be eternity. One German word for eternity, *das Jenseits*, literally means "the other side." Thus the junk gives Ray passage to "the other side."

Running through this film—as through Wenders' other films—is the search for home, which is also a search for identity. Wenders includes the clip from *The Lusty Men* in which the Robert Mitchum character comes back to his childhood home in *Lightning* and tells Ray, "It's more about coming home than anything I've seen." It's the scene, of course, that he had copied in *Kings*. Ray, whose personal slogan, a line from *Johnny Guitar,* was "I'm a stranger here myself," expresses his own longing for home in the diary: "[I had] the wildest urge to recognize and accept the face of my mother." The film implies that death is home for the homeless and at the same time the end, perhaps even the fulfillment of the search for identity, the quest for self-realization. "I have one action, which is to regain my self-image," Ray tells Wenders. "You have to select your own action."

"My action is going to be defined by yours," Wenders replies. He leaves his identity open like the characters in his earlier films who discover their identities in the flux of travel or define them in terms of the needs and actions of their companions. Throughout the film Wenders' response counterpoints Ray's action. As Ray struggles to meet the demands of filmmaking, Wenders agonizes. "All I knew was that Nick was in immense pain, that it might be better to stop shooting but that nothing might be more painful for him than that," he says in the voice-over. Ray's physical pain and vulnerability are mirrored in Wenders' psychic discomfort. He never frees himself from the fear that he is killing Ray.

In replicating the first shot in *American Friend*, the first shot in *Lightning* implies a connection between Tom Ripley and Wenders, and their subsequent actions bear this out. Ripley involves Jonathan, dying of leukemia, in exploits which speed his death but also bring him to a new level of self-awareness. Likewise Wenders urges a dying man on an adventure of self-discovery. Yet the last clearly audible line in the Epilogue is Tom Farrell saying, "Would you kill someone for a great shot?" Ripley manipulates Jonathan, and Wenders is haunted by the fear that he may be using Ray. One thinks of his rationale for using directors in the gangster roles in *American Friend*: "The only men that conduct their lives like the mafia are directors. Samuel Fuller killed an actor and two stuntmen during a shoot because he had them do something that was too dangerous."[6] Gangsters and directors both manipulate others; thus Jonathan is manipulated on screen by men who are paid to manipulate people "for great shots" off-screen. Wenders is all too aware that he, too, is a director, and like Ripley, who is torn between self-interest and a growing affection for Jonathan, Wenders is torn between being a director and being a friend. "I was more and more under the pressure of making 'a movie' . . . preoccupied with the work itself . . . rather than being concerned with Nick." When Wenders returns during the Kafka sequence, we hear the dissonant chords from *American Friend* as Ray turns to greet him, and this stresses the danger he feels he poses for Ray.

The chords recur while Wenders is reading from Ray's diary, a sequence which includes particularly Wendersian images, the silhouette of a man (Wenders) in the back of a car, and a plane wing photographed from inside the plane, as though Wenders were combining his signature with Ray's. "Since what early age have I wanted to die?" he quotes Ray. "Perhaps not die but experience death? To experience death without dying seemed like a natural goal for me." Jonathan in *American Friend* shares Ray's fascination with death, his own to begin with, and the fascination eventually works itself out in murder, which gives him the only power he will ever have over life and death.

Wenders is also drawn to death as a motif. Accidental death, murder, attempted murder, suicide, and attempted suicide pepper his films from *Same Player Shoots Again* to *American Friend*. Suicide is often linked with suffocation. In *Wrong Move* the industrialist, oppressed by loneliness, hangs himself. The plastic covering everything in his home is a visual image of suffocation. In *Kings*, in which there are many references to death and dead ends such as the mountain called "Dead Man" that Robert finds on the map, a young man's wife has committed suicide by driving into a tree. She too suffered an overbearing sense of suffocation. Her husband explains: "We were in this hotel for a few days—a small village— she said, 'It stinks, the bed stinks, the washbasin stinks, the kitchen stinks, the lamp stinks,' then all of a sudden, the smell from the kitchen—she didn't want to go on."

When Jonathan considers suicide in *American Friend*, he puts the gun to his head but first covers his head with a pillow, a visual image of suffocation if not the intended means of death. The linking of suicide and suffocation implies that these characters kill themselves because they cannot transcend the suffocating circumstances of their lives, imaged in *Kings* and *American Friend* by the circle and the maze. No passage is suggested and no self-realization, only defeat.

By contrast both Jonathan and the hero of *Alabama* die while driving. (The woman in *Kings* dies because and after her car hits a tree, not while she is still driving.) Driving is Wenders' recurrent image for what he values most: travel, change, movement, and the possibility of self-discovery. These protagonists die, but their cars keep moving, at least for a short time afterward, which suggests a momentum which death does not stop, a confrontation instead of a capitulation, and, like the junk, a passage—reinforced in Jonathan's case by the fact that he dies by the sea. Their deaths are comparable to that of Ray, who confronts death, whose ashes are carried out to sea by the junk, and who has been implicitly compared to Jonathan because of Wenders' role as Ripley.

Each of these deaths characterized by confrontation and passage is accompanied by a dramatic reference to light. In *American Friend* there is a fiery explosion on the beach just prior to Jonathan's death. In *Alabama* a few lights continue to burn in the darkness until the aperture is closed completely while the soundtrack plays the Rolling Stones' "Carry the Lantern High." In the Epilogue to *Lightning* one of the crew members suggests burning down the junk; another, in response, holds up a lighted match in front of the camera, which records the flickering dying flame as it consumes the match stick. The light suggests self-realization and transcendence.

In thus linking the hero of *Alabama,* Jonathan, and Ray, Wenders again suggests the connection between directors and gangsters. Jonathan and the hero of *Alabama* have both killed other men—not in self-defense, but in acts of cold-blooded murder. The transcendence their deaths imply comes at a cost to other men and has Nietzschian dimensions. The film director too exercises a certain God-like power, both with respect to the fiction world he creates in his films and, as Wenders points out, occasionally with respect to the real world, too. Ray's desire to know death is a wish for what is beyond human capacity, the artist's desire to appropriate God's prerogatives, as implied by the Orpheus legend. In *Alabama, American Friend,* and *Lightning,* Wenders implies that the human spirit survives largely by amoral means.

Back on the West Coast, Dennis O'Flaherty finished a screenplay for *Hammett* which the distributor greeted as "incomprehensible, unexplained, surreal."[7] O'Flaherty rewrote until one week before shooting began in February 1980. Wenders shot for ten weeks, rough-cut the film, and screened it for Coppola in August. Coppola wasn't happy with the ending but told Wenders to fine-cut the first 90 percent of the film. A fourth writer, Ross Thomas, was hired to write a new ending, and reshooting was postponed until February because Coppola needed *Hammett* star Frederic Forrest for his new film *One from the Heart*.

Wenders went back to Europe for the interim. Pierre Cottrell was producing a film called *The Territory* for Chilean director Raoul Ruiz, and the production was in financial difficulty. Film stock was low and the actors and crew had not been paid for several weeks. Wenders promised to bring leftover negative from his Road Movies company in Berlin. In the meantime Zoetrope called and informed him that *One from the Heart* was running over schedule and the *Hammett* shoot would be postponed until April. Dispirited, Wenders left for Portugal with the additional negative. Walking on the beach one day he happened upon a deserted hotel, a would-be heir to the deserted mansions and decrepit buildings that appear in many of his films, and the idea for a movie came to him. Pierre Cottrell and his *Territory* colleague Paulo Branco were enthusiastic about the idea; Chris Sievernich sold enough distribution rights to the project for production to begin two weeks later using the stranded cast and crew from *Territory,* among them Henri Alekan, celebrated cameraman for Jean Cocteau's *Beauty and the Beast.*

The resulting film, *The State of Things,* was more obviously self-referential than anything Wenders had yet done. In the pressbook for the film he included lines from the beginning of the *Inferno,* which Dante had written at the age of 35: "In the middle of life's journey / I found myself in an obscure forest / Because I had lost the right road."[8] Wenders was also 35 and wondering if he would ever be taken seriously as a filmmaker again. ("A lot of my friends in Germany, and certainly a lot of the press, thought I was more or less fucked."[9])

Inspired by the plight of the crew and actors from *The Territory, The State of Things* portrays a film crew stranded in Portugal while working on a science fiction film called *The Survivors,* a remake of Allan Dwan's *The Most Dangerous Man Alive* (1961). American producer Gordon (Allen Goorwitz) has gone back to Hollywood to solicit more money. When the last shred of film stock has been exposed, production comes to a halt. After days of waiting with no word from Gordon, German director Friedrich Munro (Patrick Bauchau) flies to Hollywood to find him.

A vehicle for exploring European versus American values in filmmaking, *The State of Things* was shot in black-and-white and divided into three distinct parts. It begins with a sequence from *The Survivors.* Only when it ends does the audience become aware that it is a film within the film. In a series of vignettes, the film's second part shows the idle cast and crew stranded in Portugal. In the third part, Friedrich searches for Gordon in Hollywood. The second and third parts of the film create a dialectic between Hollywood and non-Hollywood filmmaking through dialogue, narrative construction, and stylistic effects while the first part, the *Survivors* segment, exhibits an amalgam of European and American filmmaking styles.

A science fiction thriller, *The Survivors* takes a traditional Hollywood genre as its point of departure. Accompanied by Jürgen Knieper's dirge-like music, however, it moves at a funereal pace with sparse dialogue. The camera caresses

The State of Things (1982)
A shot from the film within the film, *The Survivors*.
(Courtesy Gray City, Inc.)

and studies the barren landscape, creating a haunting, poetic atmosphere. Quoting his own filmmaking practices, Wenders thus infuses a Hollywood genre formula with modern music, slow pacing, a poetic camera, and a tendency towards silence.

In the film's second part, German director Friedrich takes the side of non-Hollywood filmmaking and concerns himself primarily with two representative issues: the use of black-and-white film stock and the inclination not to tell stories, two of Wenders' particular predilections. "Stories only exist in stories, whereas life goes on in the course of time without the need to turn out stories," Friedrich tells the cast and crew, justifying his film's lack of a cohesive plot. To emphasize the sentiment, Wenders shows the actress Anna (Isabelle Weingarten) writing Friedrich's words, in close-up, on her napkin. Later she takes the napkin out and reads the words to herself. The fey and comic Robert (Geoffrey Carey) takes the other side and tells Friedrich, "You know Fried Rice, about your speech last night: life without stories isn't worth living!" (One is reminded of the alienated Hollywood director in Preston Sturges' *Sullivan's Travels* who concludes, "There's a lot to be said for making people laugh. That's all some people have.")

Wenders obviously identifies with Friedrich and even gives Friedrich a filmography that parodies his own. When Friedrich remarks that life goes on "in the course of time," the reference, of course, is to the German title of *Kings of the Road: Im Lauf der Zeit* ("In the Course of Time"). Significantly, the defense of stories goes to an American, in fact a Californian, whose exuberant, happy manner separates him from his doleful comrades. A storyteller himself, he provides the only "entertainment" in the second part of the film when he delivers his funny and fantastic monologue about growing up in California. Moreover his words—"life without stories isn't worth living"—prove prophetic when stories, or the lack of them, become a matter of life and death for Friedrich in the third part of the film.

The issue of shooting in black and white as opposed to color is first raised in a discussion between actor Mark (Jeffrey Kime), an amateur photographer, and cameraman Joe (Sam Fuller in his third Wenders film; he also has a bit part in *Hammett*).

> MARK: I never really thought in black and white before I saw our rushes. Do you know what I mean? You can see the shape of things.
> JOE: Well, life is in color, but black and white is more realistic.

Here Joe quotes Wenders almost verbatim: "I think black and white is more realistic than color. It sounds paradoxical, but that's the way it is."[10] Later Friedrich's lover Kate (Viva Auder) draws a landscape and tells her daughter: "Nature—everything is just lights and darks. . . ." Unwittingly she explains why one can see the shape of things better in black and white.

Wenders Going over a Scene with Sam Fuller for *The State of Things* (1982) (*Courtesy Gray City, Inc.*)

The State of Things (1982)
Sam Fuller in the resulting scene.
(*Courtesy Gray City, Inc.*)

In the third part of the film, producer Gordon, who is hiding out from the mob in a friend's mobile home, argues against black and white:

> GORDON: "Who the fuck makes black and white now? An ice cream parlor."
> FRIEDRICH: "Did you like it?"
> GORDON: "I absolutely loved it. But that's irrelevant at this point, my friend."

Relevant is Gordon's inability to convince two loan sharks to finance the rest of the film. "What's the matter with the color?" they ask him. "It looks like black and white." The hegemony of color cinematography is so pervasive that the sharks see defective color rather than black and white. (Wenders anticipates the colorization controversy here.)

The third part of the film also returns to the question of storytelling. The loan sharks want more plot.

> GORDON: In a funny way those fucking sharks sitting there in that screening room, they're not crazy. It's you and me—that's who's crazy. They're looking for a fucking story. They're not looking to kill me. They wanted a fucking story.
> . . . Without a story you're dead. You can't build a movie without a story. You ever try building a house without walls?
> FRIEDRICH: Why walls? The space between the characters can carry the load.[11]
> GORDON: You're talking about reality. Fuck reality. Cinema is not about life going by. People don't want to see that.

Friedrich recalls his earlier methods of making movies, ones that parallel Wenders' own: "It was the same story I was saying. . . . It was easy because I just went from shot to shot." He goes on to describe what happened to him in Hollywood: "But now I know how to tell stories, and relentlessly, as the story comes in, life sneaks out. . . . Death—that's all stories can carry. All stories are about death." Gordon agrees: "It's the biggest story in the world."

Though he voices the philosophy of Hollywood, Gordon sympathizes with Friedrich's aesthetics when he divorces them from the question of money. In contrast to the Portugal section of the film where the amiable Robert defends the value of entertainment, the third section reduces it to the taste of two loan sharks. Yet the vitality in the image of loan sharks attracts Wenders just as Hollywood filmmaking does. Friedrich apparently lacks that vitality. "I come from gamblers," Kate tells him: "I'm just too down-to-earth for you." Washed-up scriptwriter Dennis (Paul Getty III) praises Friedrich's artistic framing, but Gordon tells Friedrich, "You're one of the fucking dullest people I've ever seen at a meeting," and later characterizes him as a "deaf mute German." Coarseness, vitality, and money, seen as fundamentally American, oppose sensitivity, refinement, and culture, seen as fundamentally European, in an opposition similar to that in *American Friend.*

In addition to the dialogue, the film's narrative structure and formal elements also oppose Hollywood to non-Hollywood filmmaking. The second part of the film cuts quickly from one inconclusive, anecdotal look at cast or crew members to another. Though he creates no plot, Wenders captures perfectly the sense of desultory waiting that has overtaken these people. He hints at character but does not "reveal" it in the traditional narrative sense; relationships remain vague, only to be guessed at. One actress talks long distance several times, presumably to America, but we never know to whom she is talking, perhaps her boyfriend, husband, or parents. We know only that she seems unhappy in whatever the relationship is. Friedrich and Kate each have a child and appear to be lovers of some long standing, but the exact nature of their relationship is unclear. An actor and actress are having an affair, but we don't know if this relationship is beginning or ending. The cameraman's wife is critically ill. Why does he wait for news of her death before flying back to the U.S., especially since production has already stopped? Wenders lets his audience complete each character's story. Typically he captures incidental moments of truth. For example, the actress Anna tries to write while seated at the only available surface in her hotel room, a dressing table. Discomfited by the mirror she is forced to stare into, she shifts her position several times and finally covers the mirror with a scarf. In another sequence her lover Mark sits in his bathtub staring into space while a still camera set on a tripod photographs him; later he sinks out of sight beneath the water, creating an image of isolation, suffocation, and narcissism typical of the male heroes in Wenders' earlier films. In addition the camera dwells on exquisitely framed panoramas of the Portuguese coast while bars of Jürgen Knieper's eerie music punctuate this part of the film as they did the first part.

By contrast, in the third part of the film, the action speeds up and an actual story develops as Friedrich whips around Hollywood in his convertible to the accompaniment of rock music. Suspense, farce, musical, and melodrama combine in that order as Friedrich moves from one mysterious encounter to another, as he discovers Gordon driving up and down Hollywood Boulevard in a mobile home, when Gordon sings his satirical "Hollywood (never been a place people had it so good . . .)" and finally when the two men, in the midst of a leave-taking embrace, are gunned down outside the mobile home.

The third part of the film is as typically Wenders as the second. The rock music, driving sequences, snatches of Hollywood genres, and violent deaths are familiar from his earlier films and are as integral to his style as the painterly camerawork and meandering glimpses of passing life in the film's second part. Unusual is the way he has separated these elements from one another in *State of Things*. He marshalls those sensitive "European" elements into, appropriately, the European part of the film and reserves the Hollywood elements for Hollywood. Thus Wenders begins *The State of Things* with a sampling of his filmmaking style, then breaks the style down to examine its elements and their roots.

Given the film's self-reflexive nature, it's easy to see deliberate parallels between Friedrich/Wenders and Gordon/Coppola. When Friedrich's filmography flashes on Gordon's home computer, one reads the titles: *Schauplätze,* first (lost)

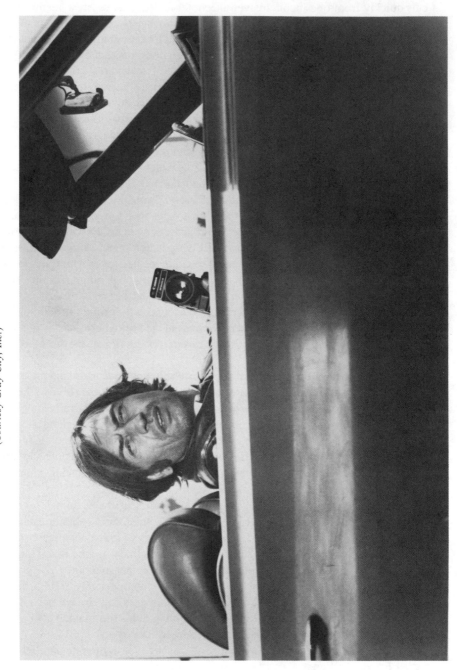

The State of Things (1982)
Friedrich (Patrick Bauchau) searches for Gordon.
(Courtesy Gray City, Inc.)

The State of Things (1982)
Gordon (Allen Goorwitz) in his mobile home.
(*Courtesy Gray City, Inc.*)

film; *Tremor of Forgery,* the Highsmith book he wanted to film but couldn't get the rights to, which appears on the theater marquee in *Goalie; Trap Door,* an aborted project for MGM; and *American Hunter,* a parody of *American Friend.* Gordon's computer, which scriptwriter Dennis tells us has the whole film on it, undoubtedly refers to Coppola's efforts to design his films on computer before shooting them. John Hoberman has suggested that the mobile home in which Friedrich finds Gordon may refer to the van from which Coppola shot *One From the Heart*[12] (although *Kings'* Bruno also lives in a van). More specific is Gordon's reference to the Chateau Marmont, a Los Angeles hotel owned by Coppola ("I had my choice of twenty-five directors sitting around the Chateau Marmont"). Yet when asked whether Friedrich is supposed to be a portrait of himself, Wenders replied, "The director Friedrich is not me; he's half of myself. And the other half is certainly Gordon."[13] Indeed, if Wenders sees himself as an amalgam of European and American filmmaking styles, he may also see himself as an amalgam of the sensitive European artist and the practical, driven Hollywood director.

Wenders reflects further on his roots in the references he makes to John Ford, Fritz Lang, and F. W. Murnau, directorial father figures familiar from his previous films. Lang and Murnau are no longer just lost German film fathers whose legacy Wenders feels cheated of. Now they represent the immigrant German director at the mercy of Hollywood. About Lang's American films he said, "It's disturbing to see the progressive assimilation and the gradual loss of what was *himself* in his films. Cinematographically I think that . . . his American films are better. . . . But at the same time, it's terrible to see what he gave up."[14]

In the film, Friedrich steps over Lang's star in the sidewalk on Hollywood Boulevard. He's nicknamed Fritz, diminutive for Friedrich, the name he also shares with Friedrich Wilhelm Murnau. His surname Munro is an anagram for Murnau. He quotes a line Murnau wrote from Tahiti in a letter to his mother when he says into a telephone answering machine, "Remember, I'm at home nowhere, in no house, in no country."[15]

John Ford is evoked through his film *The Searchers,* which appears on a theatre marquee in Hollywood. Again the theme is homelessness. In Portugal, Friedrich gives Alan LeMay's book *The Searchers* to Anna, who reads aloud, "He had no home to which he could ever go back." Like the LeMay/Ford heroes, Friedrich is a homeless searcher. He searches for Gordon and, as Wenders' alter ego, he searches for a rapprochement between two ways of filmmaking. Ultimately Friedrich the searcher is also linked to Hammett, the detective. "The myth of the detective," said Wenders, "this man who searches . . . is somehow right in the center of cinema and filmmaking for me."[16] Hammett is also a character who, like Friedrich, is searching for his identity as an artist. At least that's how Wenders envisioned him.

The *Hammett* shoot resumed in April. Wenders shot 90 pages of new script in four weeks. Less than 30 percent of the original footage was retained in the final film.

Wenders during the Filming of *The State of Things* (1982)
(*Photograph by Joyce Rudolph, courtesy Gray City, Inc.*)

Wenders noted that the first version concentrated more on Hammett's life and had the rhythm of his life; the second version had the rhythm of his fiction.[17] In other words, Hammett the questing artist had disappeared.

The story takes place in San Francisco in 1928. Hammett (Frederic Forrest), once a professional detective, has quit to become a writer, and his Continental Op stories are featured in pulp magazines. As the film begins he writes the end to another Op story. Former colleague Jimmy Ryan (Peter Boyle) drops in to ask his help in locating a Chinese girl named Crystal Ling. Ryan, the agent who trained Hammett, has recognized himself as the model for Hammett's Continental Op and expresses his annoyance. Hammett reluctantly agrees to help him, and the two head for Chinatown, where Hammett loses Ryan. Eventually Hammett discovers that Crystal Ling, former child prostitute, is at the center of a blackmail scam and that Ryan has thrown in with her. In the final confrontation, Crystal kills Ryan and escapes with ransom money that Hammett delivers for the return of photographic negatives showing the city's most prominent citizens in compromising circumstances. Disillusioned, Hammett returns home and begins a novel with a new hero: Sam Spade, based on himself.

In keeping with Tom Pope's original plan, the film is filled with references to *The Maltese Falcon* to suggest that the adventure related in the film inspired Hammett's first novel. Throughout the film, Hammett's friends call him "Sam"—his full name was Samuel Dashiell Hammett—and this underscores his connection to Sam Spade. Most of the references, however, refer not simply to Hammett's book, but to John Huston's film by the same name. The Maltese Falcon itself, looking just as it did in Huston's picture, sits on Hammett's desk. The characters of Gutman and Wilmer appear as Hagedorn and Winston, the lawyer who represents the blackmailed tycoons and his hoarse, inept bodyguard, who tails Hammett through Chinatown. Hagedorn is bald as was Sydney Greenstreet, who played Gutman in the film, whereas Hammett's original Gutman has dark, curly hair. Elisha Cook, who played Wilmer in Huston's film, plays an aging cabbie and friend of Hammett. Crystal Ling as the femme fatale is presumably the model for Brigid O'Shaughnessy. Vincent Canby calls her "a sort of Oriental Mary Astor."[18] When Hammett first encounters her, light streams through venetian blinds, creating slats of light and shadow across the room just as it does when Bogart as Spade interviews Brigid in her apartment. A Ward Bond look-alike (Richard Bradford) plays a police detective sympathetic to Hammett (as the original Ward Bond character is sympathetic to Spade), and Frederic Forrest, who actually bears some resemblance to the young Dashiell Hammett, imitates Bogart's delivery. A number of key lines are lifted from the film including Hagedorn/Gutman's "I feel you have advantage of me. Truly, sir, I do." Thus a movie adventure created in the 1980s, filled with references to a movie made in the 1930s, is credited with inspiring a book written in the 1920s. Here reflexivity gets lost in anachronism.

The 30 percent of Wenders' original film remaining in the final version undoubtedly includes the opening scene in which we see Hammett writing. Wenders fills it with distorted perspectives to suggest the artist's struggle to get his ideas on paper. They include imploded views of his apartment, created with a wide-angle lens, extreme high shots of Hammett, and extreme close-ups of his typewriter as he types, some taken from underneath looking up through the keys. Tubercular, Hammett is overcome by a spasm of coughing and ends up sprawled on the bathroom floor. The scene suggests the direction Wenders would have followed had not Coppola intervened. In the last scene Hammett typing is superimposed over black-and-white images of characters from the film to illustrate Hammett fictionalizing them and ultimately turning them into 1930s movie characters—Wenders' nostalgia at its most unabashed!

Much of the rest of the film has the dense texture and amber lighting of a Coppola film without Coppola's verve. Lacking the high camp of Coppola's subsequent *Cotton Club*, *Hammett* as a throwback to the hardboiled detective genre of the 30s appears labored and bloodless. Brian Garfield summed it up:

> *Hammett* is an interesting but not fascinating example of the period-piece crime movie—a skewed 1980 view of a 1928 that existed only in pulp magazines. Perhaps the main thing wrong with it is that it is a partly satisfactory "B" second-feature movie that just happened to cost nearly $15 million. . . .[19]

As with *Scarlet Letter*, the need to create a period piece and recoup the resultant expenditures at the box office stifled Wenders to the point where he could please no one, although he is nonetheless fond of the film.

Hammett's failure, however, should not be laid entirely at Wenders' feet. He was brought into an ill-conceived project, and everything he tried to give it— Sam Shepard as an actor/screenwriter, a more metaphysical view of Hammett's metamorphosis into a writer—was rejected by his producers. "I didn't mean to make an auteur film," he told one interviewer apologetically, "but it was hard to adapt."[20] He was interested in Hammett's drive to become a writer. He had likened it to that of Wilhelm Meister in *Wrong Move* and to his own struggle to become a filmmaker.[21] His film would have been slow, introspective, and intellectual, but it might have overcome the idiocy of its origins and appealed to an art film audience. But as Chris Sievernich put it, oddly echoing Gordon in *The State of Things*, "They wanted a movie; they just weren't interested in the inner life of Wim Wenders."[22]

The extreme introspection that his years as a "studio director" on *Hammett* had elicited in *State of Things* and *Lightning* culminated in three diary films: *Reverse Angle: NYC March '82* (1982), *Chambre 666: Cannes May '82* (1983), and *Tokyo-Ga* (1985). *Reverse Angle* was Wenders' first short since *3 American LPs* and to some extent takes up where that film leaves off. Whereas *3 American LPs* praises an America Wenders had never seen with American-*like* images from the environs of Munich, *Reverse Angle* montages images of New York that reveal the crass and banal side of American culture. Wenders calls them "tourist"

Wim Wenders in Manhattan Shooting *Reverse Angle: NYC March '82*
(Courtesy Gray City, Inc.)

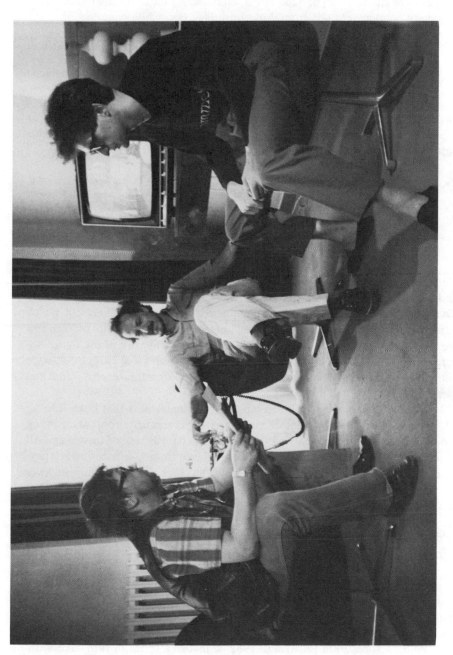

Wim Wenders with Werner Herzog and Rainer Werner Fassbinder on the Set of *Chambre 666: Cannes May '82*
(Courtesy Gray City, Inc.)

images as he shows views of 42nd Street, emphasizing the movie marquees. Subsequently he montages ads from American television while commenting:

> Another period of hostile images has started for me, and I'm running around in despair with
> my camera. . . . Contemporary American films looks more and more like their own trailers.
> So much here in America has this tendency to become its own publicity, leading to an inflation
> and invasion of mindless and despotic images. And television, as usual, the poison ivy of the eyes.

One thinks of Philip in *Alice,* writing that everything on American television is an advertisement for the status quo. The sentiment actually originates with Theodor Adorno, who wrote in 1966:

> One will have observed that it is difficult, initially, to distinguish the preview of a "coming
> attraction" from the main film for which one is waiting. This may tell us something about
> the main attractions. Like the previews and like the pop hits, they are advertisements for them-
> selves, bearing the commodity character like a mark of Cain on their foreheads. Every com-
> mercial film is actually only the preview of that which it promises and will never deliver.[23]

Wenders was indeed feeling himself forced into making such a production. He shows his editors at work on *Hammett* and a story conference with Coppola, and narrates: "I have the feeling that the story and images don't belong to me." Then he inter-cuts the mobile home sequence from *State of Things* in which Friedrich and Gordon sing "Hollywood." In the editing room a shot of Wenders from behind, standing before a window, recalls his earlier use of the figure before the window: it implies a desire to escape the strictures that Hollywood-style filmmaking has imposed on him. But he cannot. He closes the venetian blind and turns away.

Reverse Angle begins with a complaint of homelessness that links it to all of Wenders' other films. "Another night, arriving at another airport and coming from yet another city: for the first time in his life he was sick of travelling. All cities had become one." The blended cities, a theme from *American Friend;* psychic exhaustion from too much travel, one from *Alice.* The following summer Wenders directed Handke's new play *Über die Dörfer (Across the Villages)* at the Salzburg Festival. Wenders had plans to make a film from the play and spoke longingly of his desire to work again in German. He even talked of settling down in the Ruhr District: "perhaps Essen or Gelsenkirchen [the cities Alice and Philip explore in *Alice*]."[24] His youthful assertion that "identity [means] not having to have a home,"[25] was beginning to ring hollow.

The film ends with a quote from Paul Cézanne, brought to Wenders' attention by Handke's *Lesson of Ste. Victoire:* "Everything is about to disappear. You've got to hurry up, if you still want to see things." The fear that time for seeing might be running out was the inspiration for his next diary film, *Chambre 666.* At the Cannes Film Festival in 1982 he invited a series of filmmakers, including Michelangelo Antonioni, Rainer Werner Fassbinder (in his last screen

appearance), Jean-Luc Godard, Werner Herzog, Susan Seidelman, and Steven
Spielberg, into his hotel room (Chambre 666) to talk about the future of cinema.
Each participant sits in front of a tuned-in television set, which Wenders has left
running. They respond to a question Wenders has given them: "The cinema,
is it a language about to get lost, an art about to die?" along with a list of his
concerns about the threat that television poses for film. Herzog is optimistic: television has not taken him over, as he demonstrates by turning off the set. Godard's
clip is the longest, probably because he is a kind of father-figure to independent
filmmakers, but possibly because he talks at length about television. He notes
that the world of advertising is very good at saying things with one picture,
". . . like Eisenstein, as good as Eisenstein, as *Potemkin*. So commercials are
done like *Potemkin,* but *Potemkin* ran 90 minutes and an ad lasts no longer than
one minute. Because if it was any longer, you would have to tell the truth. . . ."
The filmmakers' rambling speculation on Wenders' passion and his bête noire,
film and television, testifies further to Wenders' concern about the end of cinema,
evident in his films ever since Philip picked up the newspaper obituary of John
Ford titled, "Lost World," in *Alice. Chambre 666* begins and ends with the dark
chords of *American Friend* and *Lightning over Water* that signal danger and death.
Although these films deal mainly with the death of men, the death of cinema hovers
in the background of both. *American Friend* juxtaposes early, innocent cinema
to corrupt cinema and Nick Ray's is another lost world in *Lightning*. The framing chords occur over a Lebanese cedar, which Wenders passes on his way to
the airport at Roissy. His favorite tree, he uses it to symbolize the passing time
he feels is overtaking the film industry. The tree, he notes, "has seen the entire
history of photography."

In *Tokyo-Ga* Wenders seeks another lost world, that of Ozu. He goes to Tokyo
to see if any of the timeless, measured beauty and serenity of Ozu's films still
exists. It doesn't, but Wenders is not deterred. "No other city . . . has ever felt
so familiar and so intimate to me, namely through the films of Ozu," he says,
but then acknowledges that perhaps he is only imagining it. "Perhaps I was searching for something that no longer existed." Tokyo, like New York, is a swirl of
sometimes deceptive images. For one thing, it is the television capital of the world,
and over the sets come American images. Once again Wenders registers his dis-
gust with the medium: "Every shitty television set, no matter where, is the center
of the world. . . . And here I am in the country that builds them all. . . ." He
is amused to discover Japanese teenagers enjoying a 1950s revival as they dance
to rock and roll music in the park. A substantial portion of the film is taken up
with his visit to a factory that makes the wax food that Japanese restaurants use
to advertise their menu. Fascinated by its simulation of reality, Wenders' camera
follows the preparation of the wax dishes, which, after the initial stages, is much
like the preparation of real food. He laments that the company wouldn't let him
photograph the workers eating their lunches amidst the wax food. He captures

Jean-Luc Godard in *Chambre 666: Cannes May '82*
(Courtesy Gray City, Inc.)

such a juxtaposition of image and reality elsewhere, however, when he photographs two young women standing in front of an advertisement picturing young women similar to themselves.

Wenders' interest in process, so evident in the lengthy scenes in the wax food factory, is also apparent when he curiously photographs the pachinko parlor after-hours. Westerners are always fascinated by pachinko, a vertical pinball game that sends hundreds of tiny steel balls through a maze of nails. Given all the pinball machines that appear in his early films and the pachinko parlor that appears in Ozu's *Flavor of Green Tea over Rice,* Wenders is bound to be doubly fascinated. He includes a lengthy scene in a pachinko parlor, but then returns after it closes and photographs the "nail man" who painstakingly changes the pattern of the nails in each machine so that no one will be able to memorize the patterns.

Clips from Ozu's *Tokyo Story* bracket the film, whose collage of images and reminiscences is interrupted by lengthy interviews with two of Ozu's colleagues, his alter ego actor, Chishu Ryu, and his cameraman, Yuharu Atsuta. Wenders also visits Ozu's grave. The two colleagues explain Ozu's working methods, his single-minded devotion to his art and their devotion to him. "Ozu got the best out of me, and I gave him my best," explains Atsuta. "With others . . . my best was no longer there." Atsuta begins to weep, and the film cuts to Setsuko Hara weeping at the end of *Tokyo Story.*

Two other European filmmakers appear in the film, Werner Herzog and Chris Marker, both of whom happened to be in Tokyo while Wenders was filming. Both are more poetic than Wenders and tend to carry us off into fanciful landscapes more than he does. Marker's *La Jetée* is cited: it is the name of the Shinjuku bar in which Wenders meets him. Wenders' interest in the quotidien, not poeticized but just as it is, as evidenced by the long sequence in the wax food factory, distinguishes him from Herzog and Marker, while it links him to Ozu. When Herzog suggests that one must go to outer space to find fresh images, Wenders remarks: "No matter how much I understood Werner's quest for transparent and pure images, the images I was searching for were only to be found down here below, in the chaos of the city." Ozu too drew his images and ideas from the world immediately around him, having once remarked metaphorically that he only made "tofu," a plain but nourishing food, "because I am strictly a tofu-dealer."[26]

Although *Tokyo-Ga* was made after *Paris, Texas,* Wenders least-introspective film at this writing, it rounded out the period of intense introspection and research into his roots that had begun with *Lightning over Water.* Ozu, his "only master,"[27] was sought and, to some extent, found.

8

Paris, Texas

Wenders emerged from the difficult *Hammett* years stronger than before. He had teamed up with the buoyant and practical Chris Sievernich, whom one writer calls "the most imaginative and dynamic producer on the international scene today."[1] Together they had founded a production company in New York called Gray City. *The State of Things* had been awarded a Silver Lion in Venice, Wenders' highest accolade up to that point. And from the struggles over *Hammett* (described in *State of Things*) to tell or not to tell stories, Wenders learned better how to tell stories and how to detach himself somewhat from them. This would be apparent in *Paris, Texas*.

Wenders spent the summer of 1982 directing Handke's new play *Across the Villages* in Salzburg while Sievernich looked for funding for a 250-page script Wenders had written based on the play and other recent works by Handke. But the days of German backing for difficult, intellectually demanding films were over; no one wanted to back another Wenders–Handke collaboration, and after six months Wenders dropped the project.

Wenders then began to think about collaborating with Sam Shepard on the film they had promised one another they would do together when their plans to collaborate on *Hammett* had fallen through. He had read a copy of Shepard's *Motel Chronicles* when Shepard was working on *Frances* on the sound stage next to *Hammett*'s. Wenders tried to write a screenplay from the random, frequently autobiographical sketches, but Shepard was not impressed by the results. He suggested they write a script together from scratch.

Collaborating with Shepard was a logical extension of Wenders' collaboration with Handke, for, as playwrights, both writers were rooted in the abstract, absurdist tradition of Beckett and Genet, and both prefer to describe phenomena without explaining them. A Wittgensteinian, Handke explores the net language casts over observation and behavior in *Kaspar, The Ride across Lake Constance,* and *The Goalie's Anxiety.* In these explanation becomes impossible because it, too, would be subject to the preconceptions set forth by language. Shepard, whom one always feels is dealing with the deep dark forces of human nature and society, never tries to explain these phenomena but simply exhibits the bizarre behavior they engender: Austin stealing toasters in *True West*, Tilden carrying armfuls of vegetables on the stage from an apparently nonexistent garden in *Buried Child*, Weston bringing home a grocery bag-full of artichokes to feed his family in *Curse of the Starving Class.*

The prose style of Handke and Shepard is also similar and further evidences their tendency to describe rather than to explain. In *The Goalie's Anxiety*, Handke writes:

> Bloch went back to the hotel. He found the lobby lit up but deserted. When he took his key from the hook, a folded note fell out of the pigeonhole. He opened it: it was his bill. While Bloch stood there in the lobby, with the note in his hand, the desk clerk came out of the check-room. Bloch immediately asked for a newspaper and at the same time looked through the open door into the checkroom, where the clerk had evidently been napping on a chair he'd taken from the lobby. The clerk closed the door, so that all Bloch could see was a small stepladder with a soup bowl on it, and said nothing until he was behind the desk. But Bloch understood even the closing of the door as a rebuff and walked upstairs to his room.[2]

Shepard describes a similar scene in *Motel Chronicles:*

> He got in the truck and sat for a long time without moving. He watched a green Sports Page blow across a vacant lot. Watched it catch on short sticker weeds then free itself and blow into a barbed-wire fence. Three Robins watched it too. He'd never seen Robins in this kind of weather. It troubled him deeply the way their feathers blew and they weren't even flying.
>
> When it got dark he left the truck and checked his box in the lobby. A postcard from Muskogee showing the Post Office and Federal Court House in faded yellow. . . . He poked his head into the motel bar, hoping to find Billy Wells. A fat woman holding a Chihuahua in her lap was sitting alone with a Whiskey Sour. She waved to him as though she knew him. He didn't wave back.[3]

Both writers exhibit the acuteness of observation and the exactness of description that Handke and Wenders admired in the detective fiction of Patricia Highsmith, Raymond Chandler, and, of course, Dashiell Hammett.

The similarity between Shepard and Handke is partly coincidental and partly by way of influence. According to Shepard biographer Don Shewey, Handke is one of the few fellow playwrights that Shepard reads. Shewey credits Handke's *Ride across Lake Constance* with influencing Shepard's 1974 Obie award winner *Action.*[4] *Motel Chronicles,* a collection of journal entries in the form of poems and sketches that Shepard published in 1982, is similar in form to Handke's *Weight of the World,* which is composed of chronologically arranged journal entries made between 1975 and 1977 and published in 1977. Wenders delighted in both books. *Weight of the World* served as a companion while he was making *American Friend,* and *Motel Chronicles* inspired *Paris, Texas.* Even the premise for *Paris, Texas* that Wenders and Shepard finally decided upon was anticipated by Handke. ''The idea,'' Wenders explained, ''was to have a sort of Ulysses, a man who journeys with one image in his head: a woman.''[5] In Handke's *Short Letter, Long Farewell* (c1972), the first-person hero travels across America accompanied by the vision of his estranged wife; when he finally meets her at the end of the book, the two are reconciled, not as a couple, but, like Travis and Jane in *Paris, Texas,* with themselves as human beings.

Wenders worked even more closely with Shepard on the script for *Paris, Texas* than he had with Handke on *Wrong Move.*

> We wrote on the same table. It was really something done in common. . . . There's never been such a common effort between myself and another author, because it's not generally done. There's always a competition, that is understood, between the two forms [writing and directing]. . . . With Shepard it was never so.[6]

Slowly the story evolved: a man alone on the desert, two brothers, a child, and so on. The first part of the film was securely written down, the second part was vague, and the ending hadn't been devised yet when Shepard was called away to work on *Country* with Jessica Lange. L. M. Kit Carson, father of the child hired to play the boy Hunter, helped Wenders firm up the middle part of the film; Wenders devised a scenario for the film's ending, and Shepard, still at work on *Country,* wrote the dialogue.

The film begins with desert rat Travis (Harry Dean Stanton) collapsing in a bar. His brother Walt (Dean Stockwell), a billboard designer in Los Angeles, comes to collect him, and the two head across Texas to L.A. Travis is in such a state of shock from the break-up of his marriage to Jane (Nastassja Kinski), which happened four years earlier, that he can't speak. Walt and his wife Anne have raised Travis' son Hunter (Hunter Carson); after bringing Travis to L.A., Walt manages to domesticate him somewhat and reintroduce him to his eight-year-old. To ease the tension between Travis and Hunter, Walt shows a super-8 movie he made years before on a visit to the still-married Travis. Threatened with the loss of the child she has come to love, Anne gives Travis the only clue she has about Jane's location, hoping that he will leave. Travis leaves but takes Hunter with him. He finds Jane working in a peep-show club, in which women in little cubicles talk to and act out fantasies for men who are separated from them by a pane of glass, who can see the women, but not touch them and not be seen by them. In a long monologue Travis explains to Jane (and to the audience) the reason their marriage broke up: he became insanely jealous, fantasizing that all of the time he was away at work, she was seeing other men. He brutalized her until she finally set fire to his bed one night and ran away. Awakening in time to save himself, he escaped the burning trailer and walked straight out into the desert, never looking back. Travis tells Jane that he has come to restore Hunter to her, but that he cannot stay. His sins against her have been too great, and probably he doesn't trust himself not to repeat them, for in an initial visit to the peep-show, his identity still unknown to Jane, he jealously accused her of going home with the customers.

The film weaves together the twin, though not identical, fantasies of Wenders and Shepard, just as *Wrong Move* combined elements familiar from the previous work of both Handke and Wenders. The film begins with Travis walking through

Paris, Texas (1984)
Hunter (Hunter Carson) and Travis (Harry Dean Stanton).
(Courtesy Road Movies)

Paris, Texas (1984)
Jane (Nastassja Kinski).
(Courtesy Road Movies)

the desert, which, Wenders suggests, is based on a sketch from *Motel Chronicles* in which a man burns all his belongings and walks straight out into the desert:[7]

> He drops them all on the pile of rubble. Squats naked in the baking sand. Sets the whole thing up in flame. Then stands. Turns his back on U.S. Highway 608. Walks straight out into the open land.[8]

The film also ends with this image: Travis' description of himself leaving the burning trailer that he lived in with Jane and walking straight into the desert without looking back.

Shepard used the character who lives in the desert in *True West,* a play about two brothers, Lee and Austin, who are similar to Travis and Walt. Lee lives in the desert while the college-educated Austin is a screenwriter in Los Angeles. The ultimate reference, however, is Shepard's father, who lived alone outside of Santa Fe. "My Dad lives alone on the desert," Shepard wrote in *Motel Chronicles.* "He says he doesn't fit with people."[9]

Wenders sees Travis and Walt as heirs to his Bruno and Robert in *Kings of the Road.* Bruno, the isolate who lives alone in his van, parallels Travis, while the more urbane and ambitious Robert parallels Walt. While there are no deserts in Germany, Wenders creates something close to one out of the deserted desolate landscape near the East German border.

Another Shepard device, which occurs in *Paris, Texas,* is that of having two characters change roles. In *Tooth of Crime, Angel City, Curse of the Starving Class,* and *True West,* antagonists change roles, becoming one another. In reclaiming Hunter, Travis to some extent becomes Walt, and the film underscores the identity change by having Travis dress in Walt's clothes after asking the family's cleaning woman what a "father" looks like. Walt, of course, does not become Travis, in fact he drops out of the film, so the device remains incomplete, but it echoes Shepard's earlier work nonetheless.

Travis' refusal to speak when he first meets Walt reminds one of Wenders' male protagonists in *Summer in the City, Goalie,* and *Kings,* all men of few words. Travis' pronounced eccentricity in refusing to say *anything* in the film's opening sequences is Shepard's touch, however, for his characters are much more eccentric, obsessive, and extreme than Wenders'. Soon after Travis begins speaking again, another of his eccentricities emerges: he is afraid to fly and insists on being let out of the Los Angeles-bound airplane after it begins its taxi. Again the reference here is Shepard. He refused to fly after a difficult plane trip in 1965 and relented only long enough to fly with Chuck Yeager as research for his part in *The Right Stuff.* Rabbit, the writer in Shepard's *Angel City,* is also a nonflyer.

The family created in *Paris, Texas* best illustrates the cross-fertilization of Shepard's fantasy with Wenders'. Wenders' families are always splintered, and, except for mothers and children, his characters tend to interact with peers rather than with family members, insofar as they interact with anyone. The only exceptions are Robert's confrontation with his father in *Kings* and the small nuclear family in *American Friend*. Otherwise husbands, wives, parents, grown children, and even grandparents are always separated, occasionally sought, but invariably missing. Wenders is likewise reticent to speak about his own family. In his family trilogy, Shepard, on the other hand, has created families, even extended ones, in which the bond is extremely strong despite the intense warfare that goes on between family members. Shepard frequently writes about his own family in *Motel Chronicles* and lived for many years in an extended family consisting of his wife, son, mother-in-law and her husband. The family photos that hang in the stairwell of Walt's home in *Paris, Texas* and those that Travis shows Hunter in the family album are reminiscent of the family photos Shepard includes in *Motel Chronicles,* as well as those he describes as being in the upstairs bedroom (of his grandmother's house) in both *Motel Chronicles* and *Buried Child*. Thus the separated family and the missing wife/mother correspond to Wenders' previous work while the interlinking of the two families, Walt's and Travis', and the emphasis on family ties correspond to Shepard's. The family warfare that dominates Shepard's plays has all happened in the past in *Paris, Texas* and is revealed at the end much as Dodge's crime against Halie and her last baby are revealed at the end of *Buried Child.*

Near the end of *Paris, Texas,* Travis tells Hunter that his father, also named Travis, liked to think of Travis' mother as a "fancy woman," that the joke the father liked to tell about her being from "Paris [pause] Texas," embarrassed his mother, who, Travis stresses, was *not* a fancy woman. Without being specific, Travis indicates that there was something perverse in his father's attitude toward his mother. Soon we learn that Travis too has had perverse fantasies about his wife. The implication of a moral sickness or poison passed from father to son is reminiscent of Shepard's *Curse of the Starving Class* in which the children turn out to have inherited their father's poison, his bellicose murderous personality. Wenders, too, suggests a pernicious inheritance passed from father to son in *Kings* when he implies that Robert's inability to live with his wife is related to his father's domination of his mother. However, the disorder passed down in *Kings* is a social one. As a Hitler-era husband, Robert's father was bound to dominate his family, and Robert's marriage has foundered for lack of a better model. In *Paris, Texas* and *Curse of the Starving Class,* the disorder is psychological, moral, and apparently inescapable. Shepard reflects on the inescapability of the father–son inheritance in *Buried Child* and also in *Hawk Moon,* another collection of poems and sketches, in which he writes,

I'm just amazed when I catch a glimpse of who I really am. Just a little flash like the gesture of my hand in a conversation and WHAM there's my old man. Right there, living inside me like a worm in the wood.[10]

That the perverse inheritance is only alluded to in *Paris, Texas* is probably Wenders' contribution since in *Kings* he only vaguely suggests the connection between Robert and his father, while in *Starving Class* Shepard emphatically announces the connection between the children and their father.

The desert land in *Paris, Texas* which Travis has purchased from a brochure and on which he hopes to settle with his family is reminiscent of the desert land Weston has purchased from a travelling real estate dealer in *Starving Class*. Just as that piece of land becomes an emblem for the bareness of the "starving class," so the land in *Paris, Texas* comes to stand for the perverse attitude toward women that Travis shares with his father.

Wenders' contribution here is the photograph itself, reminiscent of the many photographs in *Alice* where image was constantly compared to reality. Like the photograph of Alice's grandmother's house, the image holds out hope of a home that doesn't exist in reality.

Wenders' main contribution to the family in *Paris, Texas* is the child Hunter. Shepard does not generally feature young children in his plays or essays even though he had a growing son while he was writing most of them. Wenders, on the other hand, uses young children in large or small roles in all of his feature-length films. With his straight blond hair, cherub face, and delicate mouth, Hunter is almost identical to Yella Rottländer in *Alice*. Travis gives a strip of photomat photos of Hunter, Jane, and himself to Hunter, who studies them much as Alice studied the photomat pictures of Philip and herself. There is a lighted globe in Hunter's room reminiscent of the lighted train picture in Daniel's room in *American Friend* and like the lighted globe in Stefan's room in Handke's Road Movies-produced feature *The Left-Handed Woman*. Thus the children are not only similar but linked from film to film.

Just as Wenders' characters tend not to confront or even contact their families, they also tend to deal with one another at some remove—through pictures, notes, or by running away, as Wilhelm does in *Wrong Move* in order to be able to "love" at a distance. Shepard's characters, on the other hand, generally confront one another directly, often violently. *Paris, Texas* is full of Wendersian devices for mediating confrontations: the super-8 movie which introduces Hunter to his father (and Jane to the audience), the tentative way in which Travis wins Hunter's affection, Hunter's phone call to Walt and Anne to inform them of his decision to accompany Travis to Houston and his hanging up on them when they become angry, Travis' tape recorded farewell to Hunter, and the peep show which keeps Travis and Jane separated from one another at the end. These reflect Wenders' emotional coolness and his tendency to create only tentative, fragile bonds between characters and to emphasize their mutual isolation. Wedded to these devices for maintaining distances between characters are the stories Travis and Jane tell in the peep show, which reveal their raging temperaments and their bizarre, tempestuous actions—Shepard's stories.

Analyzing the collaboration between Shepard and Wenders, one concludes that while the two men have similar fantasies, they have opposite personalities. Where Shepard is direct and confrontational, Wenders is reticent, understated, and suggestive, and tones down Shepard's usual *Sturm und Drang*. Wenders credits Shepard with giving the film a forward thrust, which his previous films had lacked—"For once I was making a movie that wasn't meandering all over the place. That's what Sam brought to this movie . . . as an American writer: forward movement. . . ."[11] But Shepard also gave the film a new emotional depth. Wenders characterizes Travis as "less afraid" than his previous characters. "I knew I had to go further, and not tell another story of a guy who's unable to face his emotions. . . ."[12] In actual fact it was Wenders who was "less afraid" in *Paris, Texas* and Shepard who mediated the courage.

If many of the dramatic devices in *Paris, Texas* derive from Shepard, many of the images are familiar from Wenders' previous films. Trains criss-cross the desert in the early part of the film. The brothers spend the night near a car dump, reminiscent of *Goalie* and *3 American LPs*. Walt's home near the airport is reminiscent of Gloria's apartment near the airport in *Goalie,* and the gyroscope Walt plays with on his way to pick up Travis reminds one of the gyroscope Jonathan brings back to Daniel (from Paris) in *American Friend.* Travis recording his farewell message to Hunter while driving is like Ripley talking into his tape recorder while driving in *American Friend.* Whereas the tape recorder in that film looked as though it *ought* to be a walkie-talkie, in *Paris, Texas* Travis and Hunter buy real walkie-talkies, evidence of Wenders' continuing interest in communication devices. The high shot at the end of the film of Travis standing on the street corner outside the hotel where he has left Hunter looks like a painting by Edward Hopper, whose style Wenders and Müller deliberately tried to imitate in *American Friend.* Nor were film and television forgotten. In Jane's booth at the peep show, a tuned-in television fuzzes away without sound or picture as do televisions throughout Wenders' films beginning with *Goalie.* Film appears as the super-8 movie Walt shows to Travis and Hunter. More than a reflexive reference, however, it serves ingeniously as a realistically motivated flashback.

That so many images should derive unmistakably from Wenders' earlier films is not surprising since he shot the film. Surprising is the number of images that derive from Shepard yet are unconnected to the Shepardian story devices discussed earlier. For example, the film begins with a shot of a hawk looking out over the desert, reminding one of Shepard's interest in the Hopi Indian Hawk Moon legend and the eagle motif in *Curse of the Starving Class.* When Travis and Hunter stop at a motel on their trip to Houston, there is a dinosaur park behind it reminiscent of Shepard's early memory, recorded in *Motel Chronicles,* of his mother carrying him around such a dinosaur park in Rapid City, South Dakota. Later there is a shot of the moving legs of a Pegasus horse above a Mobile gas station. A similar Pegasus is included among the Johnny Dark photographs in *Motel Chronicles.*

Among the film's inevitable images are those of driving. Travis makes two car trips, from Texas to Los Angeles and back again. Driving sequences, with their shots of people in cars, shots through windshields of moving road and countryside, and exterior shots of vehicles speeding past the camera are staples of Wenders' road movies. One also associates driving with Shepard, however. A nonflyer, he frequently drives long distances. In *Hawk Moon Stories* he writes, "I've been driving for years like that. Just North. Always going North and getting nowhere. Never stopping for gas or food or sleep or friendship. Just driving."[13] When his characters are absent from the stage, they are often driving. In *Buried Child* Vince drives all night, "clear to the Iowa border."

In good *Bildungsroman* tradition, the characters of both Shepard and Wenders drive to discover themselves. But where Wenders' characters will discover in themselves a capacity for change and a need for other people, Shepard's characters discover only the bonds that tie them to their families. "I could see myself in the windshield," Vince relates in *Buried Child:*

> I studied my face. . . . As though I was looking at another man. . . . His face became his father's face. . . . And his father's face changed into his grandfather's face. . . . And it went on like that. . . . I followed my family clear into Iowa.

The journeys in *Paris, Texas* are Shepardian in that they both take Travis back to his family; they are not the free-form journeys of *Alice, Wrong Move,* and *Kings*. Travis' journey with Hunter from Los Angeles to Houston, however, expands on a theme that occurs in Wenders' earlier work, the search-for-the-mother. In *Alice* and in *Kings* the Rüdiger Vogler character searches for a mother, Alice's in the first film, his own in the second. In both cases the search implies more than the necessity of finding a specific woman; it embodies the Vogler character's longing for love. There are clear indications in *Alice* that Philip takes a personal interest in Lisa. He sniffs her pillow longingly after he discovers her missing from the hotel the morning they are all to fly to Amsterdam and looks wistfully at a picture Alice shows him of her. In *Kings* both men long for the missing women in their lives, and the failed search for Bruno's mother in the house on the Rhine island epitomizes their lack. (One remembers, too, Nick Ray's desire "to see and accept the face of [his] mother," in *Lightning*.)

In *Paris, Texas,* as in *Alice,* the hero searches for a child's mother in whom he also has a personal love interest, but unlike the resolution in *Alice,* in *Paris, Texas* we actually see him find her. The confrontation between Travis and Jane at the end of the film is considered a great breakthrough for Wenders, "the first time he has felt able to sustain a strong dramatic conversation between two central characters of the opposite sex."[14] The breakthrough is in the conversation only, however. Travis restores Hunter's mother to him, but denies himself her longed-for love. Wenders explains Travis' departure in this way:

It seemed to me that Travis had a basic responsibility to Jane and Hunter on this level: they needed each other more than his desire to possess a family. His greatest responsibility was to free Jane to accept the child—he is the only one who can "save" her, as it were. I think pretending they could get back together as a family is the biggest lie we could have told.[15]

Certainly the portrayal of sustained emotion between a man and a woman is a breakthrough for Wenders, but in both the film and in his statement, he shows himself as ignorant of women's reality as he was formerly uninterested. Jane is hardly "saved" by having Hunter restored to her. She sent him to Walt and Anne in the first place because she was unable to care for him. What has changed? She obviously has no job skills or she wouldn't be working as a quasi-prostitute. What is the addition of Hunter's needs to her monthly expenditures likely to drive her to? Hunter has enjoyed a secure, bourgeois lifestyle for as long as he can remember. How will he cope with an impoverished working mother? Obviously we are not meant to ask ourselves these questions or consider the implications of what amounts to parental kidnapping and child abandonment on Travis' part. Instead of a sociologically realistic portrayal of working class family life, Wenders has given us an allegory of sin and redemption. But the redeemed is Travis, the male hero, not Jane.

When we first meet Travis, he is in an extremely hot environment, dying of thirst, and scarred by burns. Although burns are not mentioned by name, the doctor (Bernhard Wicki) who treats him for heat prostration alludes to what we later realize are burn scars. The opening scene thus portrays Travis in a very traditional hell. Travis' meeting with Jane takes the form of a confessional with Jane, sealed off in her little booth in front of which a curtain is drawn, as the confessor and Travis as the penitent. He confesses to the sin of jealousy, one of the seven deadly. As confessor, Jane listens but does not impose penance. Travis does this himself, declaring that he has come to restore Hunter to her but cannot stay. He denies himself the only two people in the world who love him. Like Jonathan in *American Friend,* who spoke of returning to his family at the end of that film, Travis' sins bar him from the family circle (a major difference from Shepard, where family life is hell and no one is ever excluded).

As confessor, Jane is silent because she has another role to play in the allegory, that of Madonna. As such she can only forgive, not judge. Reunited in the film's penultimate scene, Jane and Hunter are the Mother and Child, symbol of promised redemption for almost two thousand years. In the last shot, Travis drives off, condemned to a kind of purgatory, but redeemed from hell. He could become a saint. Wenders' desire to create a character and find an actor who could be entirely childlike[16] suggests this potential.

Jane's role in the film is far more static than Travis'. There are two types of women in Wenders' films, real women and idea-women, and Jane is one of the latter. His real women, like Therese in *Wrong Move,* Pauline in *Kings,* and

Paris, Texas (1984)
Walt (Dean Stockwell) and Dr. Ulmer (Bernhard Wicki).
(Courtesy Road Movies)

Marianne in *American Friend,* have real needs, but Wenders quickly loses interest in them. Idea-women are the missing women in *Kings* and *Alice*'s Lisa once she becomes lost. Idea-women are longed for but never seen. An idea-woman, Jane is unique in that we see her, but we see her only as an "image." She begins as an image in Travis' mind: "A man . . . returns with one single idea, that of a woman."[17] Later she is presented as an image on a strip of photomat photos and still later as an image in the super-8 movie. When Travis finally sees her, she is still only an image in the booth. According to Wenders, "Travis is sitting in front of a screen, and she's on the screen, or behind it, and is really the object of his imagination."[18] Seen with Hunter, she is the Madonna, loving, forgiving, and lacking all human needs except that of being a mother, still only an image in a man's mind. The Christian theology and family ideology which are fundamental to this film may seem friendlier to women than the male buddy ethos and Nietzschean overtones of *American Friend,* but Wenders is a completely male-centric director here as elsewhere.

If *Paris, Texas* did not alter Wenders' ambivalence toward women, it did resolve his ambivalence toward America.[19] Although the film was not officially an American production (because financed in Europe), Wenders in many ways fulfilled his fantasy of becoming an American director with it more than with *Hammett.* Although he says he is grateful to have experienced the studio conditions under which so many of his American director heroes worked, the work on *Hammett* must have announced to Wenders everyday that he was a European and *not* an American director. Conversely on *Paris, Texas* he worked with a quintessentially American writer who nevertheless had similar sensibilities to his own. Together they created an American story, with American characters in an American landscape that had caught Wenders' imagination long before he ever dreamed of directing movies. One need only remember the simulated "American" landscapes in *3 American LPs* to realize the depth of his fascination with this landscape.

The film also marked Wenders' first attempt to break out of the insistent reflexivity, references to films and filmmaking, that had characterized his style up to that point.

> I knew at the end of *The State of Things* there was no other way out for me. I had to look at what I was trying to tell and tell it without trying at the same time to reflect the way I was telling it. . . .
>
> . . . I think that's a really serious dead end for something that I love very much, which is movies. . . . at the end of *The State of Things,* there was no other choice than to redefine, or find again, or rediscover what this is: to film something that exists, and film something that exists quite apart from movies.[20]

With *Paris, Texas* Wenders gave himself over to recapturing that innocence in cinema that at the time he made *American Friend* and *Chambre 666* he felt was so irrevocably lost. He claims that he and Robbie Müller, "for each and every shot . . . never thought of anything we'd seen before.''[21] That he quite often copied himself was, of course, inevitable.

Perhaps being forced to tell a story in *Hammett* helped Wenders to overcome a self-consciousness about narration which might, as much as the muse of modernism and his love of movies, have induced the reflexivity of his previous style. He says that *State of Things* resolved his love–hate relationship with narrative.[22] Whether due to Shepard, Coppola, or his own resolve, *Paris, Texas* is narrated far more straight-forwardly and far less self-consciously than any previous Wenders feature.

The innocence he looked for in Harry Dean Stanton as Travis may also have derived from his desire for the film to take a fresh start. Even the Catholicism that informs the film derives, one assumes, from Wenders' own period of innocence when, before the age of 16, he wanted to become a priest.

Paris, Texas won the Golden Palm in Cannes and brought Wenders his first real fame in the United States outside the small group of German film aficionados who have followed his career since the mid-1970s. These triumphs were shadowed, however, by a dispute with Filmverlag over distribution procedures for the film. Filmverlag planned to initiate distribution with only forty copies despite the success at Cannes. Wenders' Road Movies demanded that twice that many copies be put into distribution in Germany and tried to break its contract with Filmverlag. Road Movies went to court but was unable to break the contract. Further lawsuits followed as the dispute degenerated into a bitter personal battle between Wenders and the company he had helped to found. The dispute invaded German newspapers and talk shows, culminating in a three-way exchange of rhetoric in the *Süddeutsche Zeitung* between Wenders, Rudolf Augstein, publisher of *Der Spiegel* and Filmverlag's financial backer, and critic Peter Buchka, who asked if Filmverlag could still be saved (for its original purpose).[23] For although Wenders kept losing in court, he was claiming a moral victory with the public and the press, who blamed Filmverlag for its rigidity and lack of responsiveness to the very filmmakers it had been designed to aid. Indeed Augstein became so soured by the dispute that he pulled out of Filmverlag, which then merged with another distributor to become Futura–Filmverlag.

Paris, Texas, which was scheduled to open in July 1984, did not open until January 1985, when the dispute with Filmverlag was finally settled. In the meantime Germans had become so eager to see the film that they chartered buses to take them to Switzerland, where the film had already opened.

Paris, Texas brought Wenders full circle on many issues that had run through his life and work since the late 1960s. He went from a preference for the "missing story" to an acceptance of narrative; from an infatuation with America to an ambivalent love–hate for it to an acceptance; from the innocent eye of a *Sensibilist* to an almost jaded reflexivity back to a stance of innocence in his filmmaking practice. As a young unknown, he had formed a filmmakers' cooperative only to become embroiled in a bitter dispute with it fifteen years later, a measure of the degree to which circumstances for both had changed. He had completed two cycles of films; the first, made in Germany, explored the consciousness in crisis of the young German male born after World War II; the second, made in the U.S., explored his own relationship to image and narrative. The movies, America, and the lonely male were the themes that bound the two cycles together.

In the fall of 1985 Wenders returned to Berlin to work out of his Road Movies office. In the spring of 1987 he completed his first German-language feature in ten years, *Der Himmel über Berlin (The Sky over Berlin)*. Not quite the science fiction film that Wenders has longed to make, the film is about angels mixing in human affairs in the tradition of *It's a Wonderful Life* and *Heaven Can Wait*. It stars Bruno Ganz and was written in collaboration with Peter Handke. Winner of the Best Director Award at Cannes, the film promises to be the beginning of a new cycle of Wenders films.

As Wenders' career continues one expects the same measure of continuity and change that have characterized it up to now. His is the view through the window of a moving car—the films flow from one to the next, always connected, but each with a slightly altered view. His career has not been built on meteoric genius or on lucky breaks but on an incredible tenacity in the face of difficult obstacles, not the least of which was his extreme introversion and shyness. His greatest strength has been his openness to change, which also informs both the philosphy and the style of his films. It is his vision, his legacy, and his connection to Ozu.

Appendix A

Filmography

1966–67   *Schauplätze*
16mm, black and white, 10 min.
Produced, directed, photographed, edited by Wim Wenders.
Music by Rolling Stones.

Film no longer extant.

1967–68   ***Same Player Shoots Again***
16mm, black and white negative, colored, 12 min.
Produced, directed, written, photographed, edited by Wim
     Wenders.
Music: "Mood Music."
Cast: Hanns Zischler.
Shot in summer 1967. Cost: 1200 DM.

1968–69   ***Silver City***
16mm, Eastman color, 25 min.
Produced, directed, written, photographed, edited by Wim
     Wenders.
Music: "Mood Music."
Shot in summer 1968 (Munich). Cost: 2800 DM.

Re-cut as *Silver City Revisited.*

1968–69   ***Alabama: 2000 Light Years***
35mm, black and white, 22 min.
Produced by Hochschule für Fernsehen und Film, Munich;
     Production Director: Wim Wenders.
Directed, written, edited by Wim Wenders.
Photographed by Robbie Müller and Wim Wenders.
Music by Rolling Stones, Jimi Hendrix, Bob Dylan, John Coltrane.
Cast: Paul Lys (hero), Peter Kaiser, Werner Schröter, Schrat, Muriel
     Werner, King Ampaw, Christian Friedel (friends).
Shot in November 1968. Cost: 3000 DM.

1969   *3 American LPs* (*3 amerikanische LPs*)
16mm, Eastman color, 15 min.
Produced by Hessischer Rundfunk, Frankfurt a.M.; Production Director: Wim Wenders.
Directed, photographed, and edited by Wim Wenders.
Written by Peter Handke.
Music by Van Morrison, Creedence Clearwater Revival, Harvey Mandel.
Wenders and Handke appear briefly driving a car.
Shot in summer 1969 (Munich). Cost: 5000 DM

Intended for television but never broadcast.

1969–70   *Polizeifilm* ("Film about the Police")
16mm, black and white, 12 min.
Produced by Bayerischer Rundfunk, Munich; Production Director: Wim Wenders.
Directed, photographed, edited by Wim Wenders.
Written by Albrecht Göschel.
Cast: Jimmy Vogler (demonstrator), Kasimir Esser (policeman).
Shot in autumn 1969 (Munich). Cost: 1000 DM.

Intended for television but never broadcast.

1970–71   *Summer in the City* (*Dedicated to the Kinks*)
16mm, black and white, 125 min.
Produced by Hochschule für Fernsehen und Film, Munich; Production Director: Wim Wenders.
Directed, written by Wim Wenders.
Photographed by Robbie Müller.
Edited by Peter Przygodda.
Sound by Gerd Conrad.
Music by Kinks, Lovin' Spoonful, Chuck Berry, Gene Vincent, Troggs, Gustav Mahler.
Cast: Hanns Zischler (Hans), Gerd Stein (gang member who picks Hans up outside prison), Muriel Werner (gang member), Helmut Färber (himself), Edda Köchl (friend in Munich), Wim Wenders (friend at pool hall), Schrat (Christian, the rock musician), Libgart Schwartz (girlfriend in Berlin), Marie Bardischewski (friend in Berlin). Characters use their own names except where indicated.
Shot in December 1969 and January 1970 (Munich, Berlin). Cost: 15,000 DM.

1971–72   *The Goalie's Anxiety at the Penalty Kick (Die Angst des Tormanns Beim Elfmeter)*
35mm, Eastman color, 101 min.
Produced by Filmverlag der Autoren (PIFDA), Munich; Österreichischen Telefilm AG, Vienna; Production Director: Peter Genée.
Directed by Wim Wenders; assisted by Veith von Fürstenberg.
Written by Wim Wenders after book by same title by Peter Handke; dialogue by Wim Wenders and Peter Handke.
Photographed by Robbie Müller; assisted by Martin Schäfer.
Edited by Peter Przygodda.
Sound by Rainer Lorenz and Martin Müller.
Music by Jürgen Knieper; songs by Johnny and the Hurricanes, Tokens, Ventures, Roy Orbison.
Technical Direction by Honorat Stangl, Hans Dreher, Max Panitz, Volker von der Heydt.
Design by R. Schneider Manns-Au and Burghard Schlicht.
Cast: Arthur Brauss (Joseph Bloch), Erika Pluhar (Gloria), Kai Fischer (Hertha Gabler), Libgart Schwartz (Anna, hotel maid), Rüdiger Vogler (village idiot), Edda Köchl (pick-up in Vienna), Marie Bardeschewski (Marie, Hertha's waitress), Rudi Schippel (cashier in Vienna), Rosl Dorena (woman on bus), Mario Kranz (school janitor), Ernst Meister (tax assessor), Monika Pöschel and Sybile Danzer (hairdressers), Karl Krittle (castle gatekeeper), Maria Engelstorfer (shopkeeper), Otto Hoch-Fischer (innkeeper), Michael Troost (salesman at soccer match), Wim Wenders (walks through Vienna bus station).
Shot August to October 1971 (Vienna, Burgenland [Austria]). Cost: 620,000 DM.

1972–73   *The Scarlet Letter (Der Scharlachrote Buchstabe)*
35mm, Kodachrome, 90 min.
Produced by Filmverlag der Autoren (PIFDA), Munich; Westdeutscher Rundfunk (WDR), Cologne; Elias Querejeta, P.C., Madrid; Production Directors: Primitivo Alvarez and Peter Genée.
Directed by Wim Wenders; assisted by Bernardo Fernandez.
Written by Wim Wenders and Bernardo Fernandez from a script by Tankred Dorst and Ursula Ehler, "Der Her klagt über sein Volk in der Wildnis Amerika," based on *The Scarlet Letter* by Nathaniel Hawthorne.
Photographed by Robbie Müller; assisted by Martin Schäfer.

Edited by Peter Przygodda; assisted by Barbara von Weitershausen.
Sound by Christian Schubert.
Music by Jürgen Knieper.
Design by Manfred Lütz and Adolfo Cofino.
Technical Direction by Thomas Schamoni.
Cast: Senta Berger (Hester), Hans Christian Blech (Chillingworth),
Lou Castel (Dimmesdale), Yelena Samarina (Hibbins), Yella Rott-
länder (Pearl), Rüdiger Vogler (sailor), William Layton (Belling-
ham), Alfredo Mayo (Fuller), Angel Alvarez (Wilson), Rafael
Albaicin (Indian), Laura Currie (Sarah), Tito Garcia (beadle),
Lorenzo Robledo (ship captain), Jose Villasante (shopkeeper).
Shot August to October 1972 (El Ferrol and Madrid [Spain],
Cologne). Cost: 850,000 DM.

1973–74   *Alice in the Cities* (*Alice in den Städten*)
16mm, black and white, 110 min.
Produced by Filmverlag der Autoren (PIFDA), Munich, West-
deutsche Rundfunk (WDR), Cologne; Production Director: Peter
Genée.
Directed by Wim Wenders; assisted by Mickey Kley.
Written by Wim Wenders and Veith von Fürstenberg.
Photographed by Robbie Müller; assisted by Martin Schäfer.
Edited by Peter Przygodda; assisted by Barbara von Weitershausen.
Sound by Martin Müller and Paul Schöler.
Music by Can, Chuck Berry, Canned Heat, Deep Purple, Count
Five, Stories, Gustav Mahler.
Technical Direction by Honorat Stangl.
Cast: Rüdiger Vogler (Philip Winter), Yella Rottländer (Alice), Lisa
Kreuzer (Lisa, Alice's mother), Edda Köchl (Angela, girlfriend in
New York), Didi Petrikat (woman at the beach), Hans Hirsch-
müller (policeman who finds Alice), Sam Presti (used car dealer),
Ernst Böhm (writers' agent), Mirko (boy by the jukebox), Lois
Moran (ticket agent), Sibylle Baier (woman), Wim Wenders (man
standing at jukebox).
Shot August to September 1973 (South Carolina, New York City,
Amsterdam, Wuppertal and Ruhr District). Cost: 500,000 DM.

1974   *Aus der Familie der Panzerechsen* and *Die Insel* (**"The Crocodile
Family"** and **"The Island"**) from TV series *Ein Haus für Uns*
(**"A House for Us"**)
16mm, color, 50 min.
Produced by Bayerischer Rundfunk (BR), Munich; Westdeutsche

Werbefernsehen (WWF); Production Director: Eva Mieke.
Directed by Wim Wenders.
Written by Philippe Pilliod.
Photographed by Michael Ballhaus.
Edited by Lilian Seng.
Sound by Armin Munch.
Cast: Lisa Kreuzer (Monica), Katya Wulff (Ute), Nicolas Brieger and
Helga Trümper (Ute's parents), Marquard Bohm (zookeeper).
Shot in February 1974 (Cologne). Cost: 300,000 DM.

The TV series revolves around a *Freizeitheim* or after-school center
for children. Both segments are about a neurotic child Ute, who has
a fixation on crocodiles. Monica, the *Freizeitheim* teacher, worries
about Ute and urges her parents to get her professional help. The
story climaxes when Ute, upset by her parents' marital problems,
climbs a tree and refuses to come down. Wenders makes two walk-
on appearances in *Der Insel;* in the second he sits behind Ute and her
father while they watch his *Scarlet Letter.*

1974–75   *Wrong Move (Falsche Bewegung)*
35mm, Eastman color, 103 min.
Produced by Solaris Film, Munich; Westdeutscher Rundfunk
(WDR), Cologne; Production Director: Peter Genée.
Directed by Wim Wenders; assisted by Mickey Kley.
Written by Peter Handke, freely adapted from Goethe's *Wilhelm
Meister's Apprenticeship.*
Photographed by Robbie Müller; assisted by Martin Schäfer.
Edited by Peter Przygodda; assisted by Barbara von Weitershausen.
Sound by Martin Müller, Peter Kaiser, Paul Schöler.
Music by Jürgen Knieper, Troggs.
Technical Direction by Max Porupha, Herbert Svee, Alfred Hiebner.
Design by Heidi Lüdi.
Cast: Rüdiger Vogler (Wilhelm Meister), Hanna Schygulla
(Therese), Hans Christian Blech (Laertes), Nastassja Kinski
(Mignon), Peter Kern (Bernhard Landau), Marianne Hoppe (Wil-
helm's mother), Ivan Desny (industrialist), Lisa Kreuzer (Janine),
Adolf Hansen (conductor), Wim Wenders (man in dining car).
Shot September to November 1974 (Glückstadt, Hamburg, Bonn,
Österpai, Boppard, Eschborn/Frankfurt a.M., Zugspitze [West
Germany]). Cost: 620,000 DM. Winner of 6 *Bundesfilm* Prizes,
1975, for direction, screenplay, editing, photography, music, and
cast.

1975–76   *Kings of the Road (Im Lauf der Zeit)*
35mm, black and white, 176 min.
Produced by Wim Wenders Produktion, Munich; Production Director: Michael Wiedemann.
Directed and written by Wim Wenders; assisted by Martin Henning.
Photographed by Robbie Müller; assisted by Martin Schäfer.
Edited by Peter Przygodda.
Sound by Martin Müller, Bruno Bollhalder, Paul Schöler.
Music by Axel Linstädt and Improved Sound Ltd., Chris Montez, Christian St. Peters, Heinz, Roger Miller.
Technical Direction by Hans Dreher and Volker von der Heydt.
Design by Heidi Lüdi and Bernd Hirskorn.
Cast: Rüdiger Vogler (Bruno Winter), Hanns Zischler (Robert Lander), Marquard Bohm (man whose wife commits suicide), Rudolf Schündler (Robert's father), Lisa Kreuzer (Pauline), Dieter Traier (Robert's friend), Franziska Stömmer (female theater owner), Peter Kaiser (projectionist in Pauline's theater), Patrick Kreuzer (boy at railway station), Wim Wenders (spectator at Pauline's theater).
Shot between July 1 and October 31, 1975 (between Lüneburg and Hof, West Germany). Cost: 680,000 DM. Winner of FIPRESCI Prize, Cannes Film Festival, 1976.

1976–77   *The American Friend (Der amerikanische Freund)*
35mm, Eastman color negative II, 123 min.
Produced by Road Movies Filmproduktion, Berlin; Les Films du Losange, Paris; Wim Wenders Produktion, Munich; Westdeutscher Rundfunk (WDR), Cologne; Production Directors: Michael Wiedemann and Pierre Cottrell.
Directed by Wim Wenders; assisted by Fritz Müller-Scherz, Emmanuel Clot, Serge Brodskis.
Written by Wim Wenders, adapted from the novel *Ripley's Game* by Patricia Highsmith.
Photographed by Robbie Müller; assisted by Martin Schäfer, Jacques Steyn, Edward Lachman.
Edited by Peter Przygodda; assisted by Barbara von Weitershausen and Gisela Bock.
Sound by Martin Müller, Peter Kaiser, Max Galinsky, Milan Bor.
Music by Jürgen Knieper, Kinks.
Technical Direction by Hans Dreher, Andreas Willim, Wolfgang Dell, Tassilo Peik, Hans Otto Herbst, Ekkehart Heinrich.
Design by Heidi Lüdi and Toni Lüdi.

Cast: Bruno Ganz (Jonathan Zimmermann), Dennis Hopper (Tom Ripley), Lisa Kreuzer (Marianne Zimmermann), Gerard Blain (Raoul Minot), Nicholas Ray (Derwatt/Pogash), Samuel Fuller (Mafia boss), Peter Lilienthal (Marcangelo, killed on train), Daniel Schmid (Ingraham, killed in Metro), Jean Eustache (man in Arab restaurant), Sandy Whitelaw (American doctor in Paris), Lou Castel (Rodolphe), Andreas Dedecke (Daniel), David Blue (Allan Winter), Stefan Lennert (auctioneer), Rudolf Schündler (Gantner), Gerty Molzen (old lady), Heinz Joachim Klein (Dr. Gabriel), Rosemarie Heinikel (Mona), Heinrich Marmann (man in train with dog), Satya de la Manitou (Angie). Axel Schiessler (Lippo), Adolf Hansen (conductor), Wim Wenders (figure wrapped in plaster bandages in ambulance).

Shot October 1976 to March 1977 (Hamburg, Munich, Paris, New York). Cost: 3,000,000 DM.

1979–80   *Lightning over Water (Nick's Movie)*
35mm, color, 91 min.

Produced by Road Movies Filmproduktion, Berlin; Wim Wenders Produktion, Berlin; Viking Film, Stockholm; Executive Producer: Renee Gundelach; Production Directors: Pierre Cottrell and Chris Sievernich; Production Assistants: Becky Johnston, Tom Kaufman, Sara Nelson, Birgit Lelek, John Brooks; Production Accountant: Cid Milhado; Associate Producers: Laurie Frank and Jonathan Becker.

Directed by Nicholas Ray and Wim Wenders; assisted by Pat Kirck.

Written by Nicholas Ray and Wim Wenders.

Photographed by Edward Lachman; assisted by Martin Schäfer, Mitch Dubin, Tim Ray; video by Tom Farrell.

Edited by Peter Przygodda; assisted by Barbara von Weitershausen.

Sound by Martin Müller, Maryte Kavaliauskas, Gary Steel, Lee Orloff.

Music by Ronee Blakley.

Technical Direction by Stefan Czapsky and Craig Nelson.

Cast: Gerry Bamman, Ronee Blakley, Pierre Cottrell, Stefan Czapsky, Mitch Dubin, Tom Farrell, Becky Johnston, Maryte Kavaliauskas, Martin Müller, Craig Nelson, Nicholas Ray, Susan Ray, Martin Schäfer, Chris Sievernich, Wim Wenders (as themselves).

Shot April to August 1979 (New York City, Poughkeepsie, NY). Cost: $700,000.

1978–82   *Hammett*

35mm, Technicolor, 94 min.

Produced by Orion Films and Zoetrope Studios, Los Angeles; Executive producer: Francis Ford Coppola; Producers: Fred Roos, Ronald Colby, Donald Guest; Associate Producer: Mona Skager; Production Directors: Ronald Colby and Robert J. Huddleston; assisted by Michael Hacker and Steve Danton.

Directed by Wim Wenders; assisted by Arne Schmidt, Ronald Colby, David Valdes and Daniel Attias.

Written by Ross Thomas and Dennis O'Flaherty from an adaptation by Thomas Pope of the novel *Hammett* by Joe Gores.

Photographed by Philip Lathrop and Joseph Biroc; assisted by Robert Torres and Todd Henry.

Edited by Barry Malkin, Mark Laub, Robert Q. Lovett, and Wendy Roberts.

Sound by James Webb, Jr. and Richard Goodman.

Music by John Barry.

Art Direction by Angelo Graham and Leon Erickson.

Design by Dean Tavoularis and Eugene Lee; assisted by James Murakami and Bob Goldstein; costumes by Ruth Morely.

Technical Direction by Carl Manoogian, Pete Papanickolas, Bob Woodside and Larry Gilhouley; assisted by Clifford Dalton.

Cast: Frederic Forrest (Hammett), Peter Boyle (Jimmy Ryan), Marilu Henner (Kit Conger, Sue Alabama), Roy Kinnear (Eddie Hagedorn), Elisha Cook (Eli, the taxi driver), Lydia Lei (Crystal Ling), R. G. Armstrong (Lt. Pat O'Mara), Richard Bradford (Det. Tom Bradford), Michael Chow (Fon Wei Tau), David Patrick Kelly (the punk), Sylvia Sidney (Donaldina Cameron), Jack Nance (Gary Salt), Elmer L. Kline (Doc Fallon), Royal Dano (Pops), Samuel Fuller (old billiard player), Lloyd Kino (barber), Fox Harris (Frank), Rose Wong (laundress), Liz Robertson (woman in the library), Jean Francois Ferreol (French sailor), Alison Hong (girl), Patricia Kong (girl at Fong's), Lisa Lu (Miss Cameron's assistant), Andrew Winner (bank guard), Kenji Shibuya (Chinese bouncer), James Quinn (Fong's bodyguard), Mark Anger (barman), James Devney (projectionist), Hank Worden (poolball employee), Cicely Rush and Christopher Day (neighborhood children), Christopher Alcaide, James Brodhead, John Hamilton, Ben Breslauer, John T. Spiotta, and Ross Thomas (men in the council chamber).

Shot March to June 1980 and November/December 1981 (Los Angeles).

1981–82   *The State of Things (Der Stand der Dinge)*
35mm, black and white, 123 min.
Produced by Gray City, Inc., New York; Road Movies, Berlin; V.O.
Films, Lisbon; Executive Producer; Chris Sievernich; Associate
Producers: Paulo Branco and Pierre Cottrell; assisted by Steve
McMillin and Judy Mooradian.
Directed by Wim Wenders; assisted by Carlos Santana.
Written by Robert Kramer and Wim Wenders.
Photographed by Henri Alekan and Fred Murphy; assisted by Agnes
Godard and Steve Dubin.
Edited by Barbara von Weitershausen; consultant: Peter Przygodda.
Sound by Maryte Kavaliauskas; assisted by Jean Paul Mugel and
Morning Pastoroc.
Music by Jürgen Knieper.
Design by Ze Branco; costumes by Maria Gonzaga.
Cast: Patrick Bauchau (Friedrich), Allen Goorwitz (Gordon), Isabelle
Weingarten (Anna), Samuel Fuller (Joe), Paul Getty III (Dennis),
Viva Auder (Kate), Monty Bane (Herbert), Geoffrey Carey
(Robert), Roger Corman (Jerry), Jeffrey Kime (Mark), Rebecca
Pauly (Joan), Alexandra Auder (Jane), Camila Mora (Julia), Ar-
turo Semedo and Francisco Baiao (crew members), Martine Get-
ty (secretary).
Shot February to April 1981 (Sintra [Portugal] and Hollywood). Win-
ner of the Golden Lion, Venice Film Festival, 1982.

1982   *Reverse Angle I: NYC March '82 (Lettre d'un cinéaste; quand je
m'éveille)*
16mm, color, 17 min.
Produced by Gray City, Inc., New York; Production Director:
Lilyan Sievernich; assisted by Charles Libin.
Directed and written by Wim Wenders.
Photographed by Lisa Rinzler.
Edited by Jon Neuburger.
Sound by Maryte Kavaliauskas.
Music by Allen Goorwitz, Del Byzanteens, Echo and the Bunnymen,
Martha and the Muffins, Public Image Ltd.
Appearances by Wim Wenders, Isabelle Weingarten, Barry Malkin,
Mark Laub, Bob Lovett, Francis Ford Coppola.
Shot in March 1982 (New York City). Cost: $15,000.

Commissioned by French television Antenne II for series "Cinéma-
Cinémas."

1982–83   *Chambre 666: Cannes May '82*
16mm, Fujicolor 250, 45 min.
Produced by Gray City, Inc., New York; Production Director: Chris Sievernich.
Directed by Wim Wenders.
Photographed by Agnes Godard.
Edited by Chantal de Vismes.
Sound by Jean Paul Mugel.
Appearances by Jean-Luc Godard, Paul Morrissey, Mike De Leon, Monte Hellman, Romain Goupil, Susan Seidelman, Noel Simsolo, Rainer Werner Fassbinder, Werner Herzog, Robert Kramer, Ana Carolina, Mahroun Bagdadi, Steven Spielberg, Michelangelo Antonioni, Wim Wenders, Yilmaz Güney (voice only).
Shot in May, 1982 (Cannes, France).

1983–84   *Paris, Texas*
35mm, color, 145 min.
Produced by Road Movies, Berlin; Argos Films, Paris; Executive Producer: Chris Sievernich; Producer: Don Guest; Production Manager: Karen Koch.
Directed by Wim Wenders; assisted by Claire Denis.
Written by Sam Shepard; adapted by L. M. Kit Carson.
Photographed by Robbie Müller assisted by Agnes Godard and Pim Tjujerman; 2nd unit photography by Martin Schäfer.
Edited by Peter Przygodda assisted by Anne Schnee; sound editor: Dominque Auvray.
Sound by Jean Paul Mugel, Douglas Axtell, Lothar Mankiewicz, and Hartmut Eichgrün.
Music by Ry Cooder.
Design by Kate Altman assisted by Lorrie Brown; costumes by Birgitta Bjerke.
Cast: Harry Dean Stanton (Travis), Nastassja Kinski (Jane), Dean Stockwell (Walt), Hunter Carson (Hunter), Auroré Clement (Anne), Bernhard Wicki (Dr. Ulmer), John Lurie (Slater), Sally Norvell (Nurse Bibs), Tom Farrell (Screaming Man), Claresie Mobley (car rental woman), Socorro Valdez (Carmelita), Viva Auder (Woman on TV), Sam Berry (gas station attendant), Edward Fayton (Hunter's friend), Justin Hogg (Hunter, age 3), the Mydols (band).
Shot November to December 1983 (Texas and Los Angeles); Winner of the Golden Palm, Cannes Film Festival, 1984.

Dedicated to Lotte H. Eisner.

1984–85 *Tokyo-Ga*
16mm, color, 92 min.
Produced by Gray City, Inc., New York; Wim Wenders Produktion, Berlin; Chris Sievernich Produktion, Berlin; Westdeutscher Rundfunk, Cologne; Production Director: Chris Sievernich assisted by Lilyan Sievernich and Ulla Zwicker.
Directed and written by Wim Wenders.
Photographed by Edward Lachman.
Music by "Dick Tracy," Loorie Petitgand, Meche Mamecier, and Chico Rojo Ortega.
Appearances by Chishu Ryu, Yuharu Atsuta, Werner Herzog.
Shot in January 1984 (Tokyo).

1986–87 *The Sky over Berlin (Der Himmel über Berlin)*
35mm, black and white and color, 130 min.
Produced by Road Movies, Berlin; Argos Films, Paris; Westdeutscher Rundfunk, Cologne; Executive Producer: Ingrid Windisch; Producer: Wim Wenders and Anatole Dauman; Associate Producer: Joachim von Mengershausen.
Directed by Wim Wenders; assisted by Claire Denis.
Written by Wim Wenders and Peter Handke.
Photographed by Henri Alekan.
Edited by Peter Przygodda.
Sound by Lothar Mankiewicz.
Music by Jürgen Knieper.
Design by Heidi Lüdi; costumes by Monika Jacobs.
Cast: Bruno Ganz (Damiel), Solveig Dommartin (Marion), Otto Sander (Cassiel), Curt Bois (Homer), Peter Falk (himself).
Shot in autumn 1986. Prize for Best Director, Cannes Film Festival, 1987.

Note on Distribution Sources

Most of Wenders' films are available from Gray City, Inc., 853 Broadway, New York, New York 10003 (212-473-3600)
The American Friend is distributed by New Yorker Films, 16 West 61st St., New York, New York 10023 (212-247-6110)
Paris, Texas is distributed by Films Incorporated.

Appendix B

The Films of Peter Handke

1970   *Chronik der laufenden Ereignisse* ("Chronicle of Current Events")

Made for television (WDR), *Chronik,* whose title comes from a Soviet underground newspaper, purported to be an impressionistic image of what Handke had seen on German television between 1968 and 1969. Just as *Goalie* has been an anti-thriller and *Wrong Move* an anti-Bildungsroman, *Chronik* was an anti-television television film. Sharing Wenders' dislike of television, Handke explained the film as follows:

> *Chronik der laufenden Ereignisse* insofar as it tried to be an allegory of two years of West German history, might also be seen as an allegory of the mythical struggle between cinema and television images, in which at the end, the cinema images are suppressed by the television images. The symbol of this victory would then be the television clock, which, after it suddenly kept going [didn't gong] once in the middle of the film, gongs routinely at the end of the film.[1]

He refers to the fact that many films are shown on West German television and contrast with the television shows, many of which come from the U.S. He also refers to the clock, similar to the one that marks the time on CBS' *60 Minutes,* which appears between shows on German television and gongs on the hour. The failure of the clock to gong in the middle of the film suggests a general subversion of the established order, to which the film's opening scene refers. The titles: "Nothing has definitive value any longer; there is no accepted order anymore. All concepts of good and evil, right and wrong, true and false have been jettisoned. . . . How should one live?" appear in the film's opening shot.

Handke tries to answer his question with a quartet of actors who appropriate various heroic personalities from film and literature.

They are Sam Beaumont (Ulrich Gressieker), Philip Spade (Rüdiger Vogler), whose names are scrambled versions of the detective heroes of Dashiell Hammett and Raymond Chandler, Kelly (Didi Petrikat), after Grace Kelly, and "the girl" (Libgart Schwartz). The four interact in scenes which make no narrative sense, but *look* like movie scenes. In one, Kelly repeats for Sam Beaumont the dream that Janet Henry tells Ned Beaumont in Hammett's *Glass Key* about a house full of snakes that escape. Again the emphasis is on chaos and disorder.

If the individualism of the fictional film heroes and heroines is one answer to the chaos, the other is mediocrity and selling out, one suggested by the television images. Among these are a game show and a panel discussion. During the game show contestants must first blow up balloons and then perform a variety of ridiculous tasks before a bell sounds. Unfortunately none of the eager and frustrated players even manages to finishing blowing up his or her balloon.

The panel discussion features a number of prominent Americans, some with names of real people (Robert McNamara and Delbert Mann) and one (Robert McNamara) with his real career resumé. The film was, of course, made at the height of the Vietnam War when Robert McNamara was a key political figure. In each case, the panelists' career resumés show them studying in Germany during the 1930s and then going on to hold key positions in American public and private institutions and corporations, such as the FBI, Ford Foundation, Lockheed, and General Motors. The implication is that they learned fascism in Germany in the 30s and put their knowledge to good use in postwar America.

Having established a prewar connection between Germany and Americans in power in the 1960s, Handke suggests the continuing interdependence between like-minded politicians in Germany and the U.S. when he has "the girl," dressed in a Bavarian dirndl, passing out handbills for Senator Paul Vincent Harwood. Harwood's photograph on the handbills shows him swinging a Tirolean hat over his head.

At the end the television clock gongs properly. Order is restored in the name of mediocrity and hypocrisy, i.e., television.

The film was shot nine months after Wenders' *Summer in the City,* and Handke's and Wenders' styles are clearly related in the driving sequences, shots of cars, and many close-ups of objects, particularly gadgets such as telephones, a taxi meter, a parking meter, and the closed circuit television at an airport. Three of the actors, Libgart Schwartz, who was still Mrs. Peter Handke at this time,

Rüdiger Vogler, who had appeared in a number of Handke's theatrical premiers, and Didi Petrikat (with whom both Wenders and Handke were in love!) would appear in Wenders' later films. Libgart Schwartz had already appeared in *Summer*.

1977   *The Left-Handed Woman* (*Die linkshändige Frau*)

Commissioned by Westdeutsche Rundfunk to write *Chronik,* Handke took over directing the film only when no other suitable director could be found. Likewise he had hoped Wenders would direct *The Left-Handed Woman,* but Wenders, no doubt uneager to direct a film with a female lead, encouraged Handke to direct it himself. Wenders' Road Movies produced the film, however, and Handke used some of the Wenders team—cameramen Robbie Müller and Martin Schäfer and editor Peter Przygodda. He also used the same Eastmancolor Negative II film that Wenders had used on *American Friend.*

The film frequently pays tribute to Wenders. Toward the beginning there are shots of a train and views out of the train's window as it rushes through the countryside. A shot inside the Orly airport shows the same complex of silver escalators from almost the same angle that Wenders had used in *American Friend.* Handke also includes what is in Wenders' films almost obligatory, a trip to the photomat, and there, appropriately, the heroine Marianne meets an unemployed actor played by Wenders regular, Rüdiger Vogler. When they attempt to shake hands, an electric shock in the form of a spark jumps visibly between their hands just as it had jumped between Jonathan's hand and the television set in *American Friend.* Wenders had used the shock to jeer at television; Handke uses it to spoof the "electricity" of traditional romances as well as to comment on the inevitability of human isolation. "In the cold everything becomes electrified," apologizes Marianne.

Overall, however, the film does not have the look of a Wenders film. It is lusher, more lyrical, less harshly realistic. Robbie Müller, who exulted in the freedom Handke gave him, used yellow filters to create this lush effect and aimed, he said, for a stylized photography that would match the stylized speech.[2] Handke wanted to create "mythic" images in the tradition of John Ford[3] and to this end sometimes indulged in a broad, unsubtle symbolism as when he shows a close-up of petals falling off the tulips in the restaurant where Marianne and her husband Bruno dine the night before she asks him to leave her. Handke and Müller studied Andrew Wyeth's paintings for inspiration, and Wyeth's influence shows up in the stark, but strong, intense compositions, particularly inside Marianne's house.

Peter Handke Directs Edith Clever and Bruno Ganz in *The Left-Handed Woman* (1977) (*Courtesy New Yorker Films*)

Like Wenders, Handke was infatuated with Yasujiro Ozu. But Wenders' similarity to Ozu lay in common attitudes toward film-making while Handke quoted Ozu's film language often and directly. In one scene Marianne sits on the floor in her ironing room with her back against the wall and her head in her arms. The camera pans from her to a picture on the wall, holds on the picture, then pans back to Marianne, who now sits with her head up looking as though she had resolved something for herself. A similar move from a character in one frame of mind to an object and back to the same character in a changed frame of mind occurs in Ozu's *Late Spring* (1949) and has been celebrated by several authors.[4] Handke undoubtedly had this scene of Ozu's in mind for he not only copied the device, but used a blown-up photograph of Ozu for the picture on the wall to which his camera pans. Thus Handke acknowledged his debt to Ozu while in the act of borrowing from him.

The story, which Handke published as a novella in 1976, concerns a married German woman Marianne (Edith Clever), living in Paris with her German husband (Bruno Ganz) and preadolescent son (Markus Mühleisen). For no apparent reason, she suddenly decides she would rather live without her husband. Throughout the film various characters try to dissuade Marianne from her decision, telling her that living alone is difficult, painful, and might even lead to madness. These include a publisher (Bernhard Wicki), for whom she recommences doing translations from French into German; her father (Bernhard Minetti); and her best friend Franziska (Angela Winkler). Not happy, but enthralled with finding her own way, Marianne ignores them. Small moments—walking on stilts, watching snowflakes fall through the branches of a tree—reward her. Her husband, her publisher, and the unemployed actor all pursue her, but she insists on defining her relationship to men in a new way, of projecting herself as a whole person. This she conveys less with words than with the aura of her self-possession. (In Handkean fashion the dialogue is sparse, stylized, and always overloaded with meaning as in the quote above: "In the cold everything becomes electrified.") People are attracted to her strength. At the end her friends gather uninvited at her house. In some ways she is less alone than before, and yet she *is* alone; she is autonomous. The film ends with a quote from Vlado Kristl: "Haven't you ever noticed that there is only room for those who bring their own room with them . . . ?" To this end, Handke saw Marianne not as a feminist, but as an Everyman, an individual seeking her own space in a world which tends to put people in niches and define them in terms of their relationship to other people and society.[5]

From the time Marianne asks her husband to leave, the film follows less the course of a normal narrative than that of an assemblage of moments: short scenes in Marianne's house, visits from people, and long walks. In fact, much of the film's continuity is provided by three long walks, one which Marianne makes alone through her suburb, one which she takes with her father, and one with her son Stefan. They are like the long walk in *Wrong Move* and provide Handke with the opportunity to string his moments, his characters' random observations and comments, on a single thread without which the film would probably seem too choppy.

In addition to the influence of Wenders, Ozu, and Ford, *Left-Handed Woman* is also indebted to the French film. Although both Edith Clever and Bruno Ganz are veterans of Berlin's Schaubühne am Halleschen Ufer, their appearance in a film together can't help but recall Eric Rohmer's comedy, *The Marquise von O* (1975). *Left-Handed Woman* has whimsical touches that are not common in German films from this period. One Tati-like scene has an old couple walking in the background who peer back curiously at Bruno and Marianne while they argue on the street.

Notes

Preface

1. Hans C. Blumenberg, "Wim Wenders," *Extra,* (September 1976), p. 61. (Unless otherwise noted, all translations from German and French texts are by the author.)

2. All film titles will be those used by U.S. distributors. In many cases the original title will follow in parentheses. Titles of films not distributed in English-language versions will be given in the original language.

3. Wenders to audience in Ann Arbor, Michigan, 6 April 1978. See also Jan Dawson, *Wim Wenders* (New York: 1976), p. 19, and Hubert Niogret, "Entretien avec Wim Wenders," *Positif,* November 1976, p. 28.

4. Bernd Schwamm to author (Munich), 1 December 1979.

5. Viggo Graf Blücher, *Jugend zwischen 13 und 24,* 3 vols. (Bielefeld: 1975) 3:30ff.

6. Dawson, *Wenders,* p. 8.

Chapter 1

1. Michel Ciment, "Entretien avec Wim Wenders," *Positif,* November 1980, p. 15.

2. Ibid., p. 15.

3. Robert Joseph, "American Films in Germany—A Report," *Screen Writer,* May 1946, p. 13.

4. Lotte Eisner, *Fritz Lang,* trans. Gertrud Mander (New York: 1977), p. 384. For more on the German emigrés in Hollywood, see Jan-Christopher Horak, "The Palm Trees Were Gently Swaying: German Refugees from Hitler in Hollywood," *Image* 23:1 (1980), pp. 20–32.

5. See David Stewart Hull, *Film in the Third Reich* (Berkeley: 1973).

6. Robin Bean, "Bubis Kino," *Films and Filming,* February 1967, pp. 50–51.

7. The new German filmmakers revised the *Heimatfilm* and turned its rural, frequently historical, format into a forum for examining power structures and power relationships in society: Peter Fleischmann's *Hunting Scenes from Lower Bavaria (Jagdszenen aus Niederbayern,* 1968), Uwe Brandner's *I Love You, I Kill You (Ich liebe dich, ich töte dich,* 1971), Reinhard Hauff's *Mathias Kniessl* (1971), Volker Schlöndorff's *The Sudden Wealth of the Poor People of Kombach (Der plötzliche Reichtum der armen Leute von Kombach,* 1971), Hans Geissendörfer's *Sternsteinhof* (1976), and Josef Rödl's *Albert—Why? (Albert—warum?,* 1978) are some of the better known

examples. See Hans Günther Pflaum and Hans Helmut Prinzler, *Film in der Bundesrepublik Deutschland* (Munich: 1979), pp. 24–39, and Eric Rentschler, *West German Film in the Course of Time* (Bedford Hills, New York: 1984), pp. 109–125.

8. Jan Dawson, "A Labyrinth of Subsidies," *Sight and Sound*, Winter 1981–82, p. 14.

9. Michel Boujut, *Wim Wenders*, (Paris: 1982), p. 8.

10. Jan Dawson, *Wim Wenders* (New York: 1976), p. 20.

11. Candice Russell, "Film Maker Wenders: Endless Search," *Miami Herald*, 12 December 1976.

12. Wenders to author (Los Angeles), 1 August 1980.

13. Ibid.

14. Boujut, *Wenders*, p. 13.

15. Wim Wenders to author (Los Angeles), 2 August 1980.

16. Wolfgang Längsfeld to author (Munich), 5 February 1979.

17. Walter Adler, "Das grosse Geld, die Angst und der Traum von Geschichten Erzählen," *Filmkritik*, December 1978, p. 683.

18. Bill Thompson, "A Young German Filmmaker and His Road Movie," *1000 Eyes*, November 1976, p. 22.

19. "Kritischer Kalendar," *Filmkritik*, December 1969, p. 751.

20. "Terror der Gesetzlosen," *Süddeutsche Zeitung* (Munich), 6–7 September 1969.

21. "Easy Rider, ein Film wie sein Titel," *Filmkritik*, November 1969, p.677.

22. "Repertoire," *Filmkritik*, June 1969, p. 383.

23. "Rote Sonne," *Filmkritik*, January 1970, p. 9.

24. "Verachten, was verkauft wird," *Süddeutsche Zeitung*, 16 December 1969.

25. Fritz Müller-Scherz and Horst Wiedemann, "Wim Wenders über 'Im Lauf der Zeit,' " *Film und Ton Magazin*, May 1976, p. 54.

Chapter 2

1. Tony Rayns, "Forms of Address: Interviews with Three German Filmmakers," *Sight and Sound*, Winter 1974–75, p. 5.

2. This version is distributed in the U.S. simply as *Silver City.*

3. In his forthcoming dissertation "The Imaginary City: Theories of Urban Perception in European Culture and Social Thought" (Univ. of California, Santa Cruz), Edward Dimendberg suggests links between Wenders' early films and the work of the Situationists, a group of French avant-garde artists active in the 1950s and 60s, who took a special interest in streets, cities, and spontaneously evolving events.

4. "keine 'exprmnte,' " *Texte zu Filmen und Music* (Berlin, n.d.), p. 1; reprinted from *Film*, February 1968.

5. Jan Dawson, *Wim Wenders* (New York: 1976), p. 22.

6. See Wenders' comments on *Kings of the Road* in Fritz Müller-Scherz and Wim Wenders, *Kings of the Road*, photoscript, trans. Christopher Doherty (Munich: 1976).

7. Rayns, "Forms of Address," p. 6.

8. "Easy Rider: ein Film wie sein Titel," *Filmkritik*, November 1969, p. 675.

9. Dawson, *Wenders*, p. 12.

10. Ibid., p. 11.

11. Ibid., p. 12.

12. "Tired of Waiting," *Filmkritik*, February 1970, p. 65.

13. Ibid., p. 65.

14. Hubert Niogret, "Entretien avec Wim Wenders," *Positif*, November 1976, p. 27.

15. Dawson, *Wenders*, p. 18.

16. Rayns, "Forms of Address," p. 6.

17. The "Easter Demonstrations" of 1968 were provoked by the assassination attempt on student leader Rudi Dutschke, for which the red-baiting tactics of Axel Springer's yellow press were held ultimately responsible. (The methods of the Springer press are the subject of Heinrich Böll's novel, turned film by Volker Schlöndorff, *The Lost Honor of Katherina Blum*.

18. Donald Duck is no stranger to political discourse in Germany. In his *Left-Handed Woman*, Peter Handke has the teacher Franziska say: "That duck is the only comic book character I tolerate in my class. I even encourage my pupils to read his sad adventures. They learn more about real life from this eternal victim than they could from anyone else in this homeowner's paradise, where all existence boils down to imitating TV."

19. "Easy Rider," p. 13. Wenders' fears were not totally unfounded. By 1969 his commune had disbanded and some of its members had gone underground. Some became terrorists and were later killed.

20. Wenders to author (Los Angeles), 1 August 1980.

21. Heiko R. Blum, "Gespräch mit Wim Wenders," *Filmkritik*, February 1972, p. 71.

22. Bernd Schwamm to author (Munich), 1 December 1979.

23. Filme von Wim Wenders," *Filmkritik*, May 1969, p. 316.

24. Wim Wenders to author, 1 August 1980.

25. Dawson, *Wenders*, p. 19.

26. Ibid., p. 13.

Chapter 3

1. As of 1967 the Kuratorium was no longer financed by the federal government but by state governments on a voluntary basis. Thus Wenders was still able receive money from it in 1971. Filmverlag began as a distribution and production co-operative, but financial difficulties caused the liquidation of the production end (PIFDA) in 1974.

2. See chapter 2, n. 21.

3. Heiko R. Blum, "Blende auf, Kamera ab," *Aachener Nachrichten*, 30 October 1971.

4. *The Goalie's Anxiety at the Penalty Kick*, trans. Michael Roloff (New York: 1972), pp. 103–4.

5. Ibid., p. 57.

6. Siegfried Kracauer, *Theory of Film: The Redemption of Physical Reality* (London: 1974), p. 55.

7. Fritz Müller-Scherz and Horst Wiedemann, "Wim Wenders über 'Im Lauf der Zeit,'" *Film und Ton Magazin,* May 1975, p. 54.

8. Jan Dawson, *Wim Wenders* (New York: 1976), p. 9.

9. Ibid.

10. Ibid., p. 8.

11. For a more detailed analysis of the connection between Ozu and Wenders see my "West Looks East: The Influence of Yasujiro Ozu on Wim Wenders and Peter Handke," *Art Journal,* Fall 1983, pp. 234–39.

12. Dawson, *Wenders,* p. 8.

13. Jeanine Meerapfel, "Komm, Keule, wir drehn ein heisses Bild," *Die Zeit Magazin,* 1 July 1977.

Chapter 4

1. Jan Dawson, *Wim Wenders* (New York: 1976), p. 7.

2. Wim Wenders to author (Los Angeles), 1 August 1980.

3. Heiko R. Blum, "Die Verfemte von Salem," *Der Taggesspiegel* (Berlin), 11 March 1973.

4. Dawson, *Wenders,* p. 22.

5. "Wildwestliche Einfaltspinselei," *Die Stuttgarter Zietung,* 15 March 1973.

6. Dawson, *Wenders,* p. 22.

7. Edward Lachman, Peter Lehman, and Robin Wood, "Wim Wenders: An Interview," *Wide Angle* 2:4 (1979), p. 78.

8. Carna Zacharias, *Abend Zeitung* (Munich), 29 July 1977.

9. Dawson, *Wenders,* p. 4.

10. "Die Männer dieser Generation," *Filmreport* 5–6, 1976.

11. "Wim Wenders, a Worldwide Homesickness," *Film Quarterly,* Winter 1977–78, p. 11.

12. Wim Wenders to author (Los Angeles), 2 August 1980.

13. Blum, "Verfemte."

14. Michel Ciment, "Entretien avec Wim Wenders," *Positif* no. 236 (November 1980), p.16.

15. Ibid., p. 15.

16. "The Myths about America: Origins and Extensions," in Alexander Ritter (ed.), *Deutschlands literarisches Amerikabild* (Hildesheim: 1977), pp. 37–45.

17. *Germany Rediscovers America* (Tallahassee: 1968), p. 59.

18. Cf. Eric Rentschler, "How American Is It: The U.S. as Image and Imaginary in German Film," *Persistence of Vision,* Fall, 1985, pp. 5–18.

19. Alain Masson and Hubert Niogret, "Entretien avec Wim Wenders," *Positif,* October 1977, p. 24.

20. Ibid., p. 24.

21. David Sterritt, "German Director in U.S. Tradition," *Christian Science Monitor,* 15 January 1979.

22. New Yorker Films, *The American Friend,* promotion brochure.

23. Dawson, *Wenders,* p. 19.

24. Wim Wenders, telex to PIFDA, 17 November 1972 (archives, Filmverlag der Autoren, Munich).

25. Fritz Müller Scherz and Wim Wenders, *Kings of the Road,* photoscript, trans. Christopher Doherty (Munich: 1976).

26. Terry Curtis Fox, "Wenders Crosses the Border," *Village Voice,* 3 October 1977.

27. Dawson, *Wenders,* p. 12.

Chapter 5

1. Quoted by Friedrich in *The State of Things* from a letter by F. W. Murnau. See Lotte H. Eisner, *Murnau* (Berkeley:1973), p. 13.

2. *The Bildungsroman from Wieland to Hesse* (Princeton: 1978), pp. 35 and 72.

3. *West German Film in the Course of Time* (Bedford Hills, N.Y.: 1984), p. 178.

4. Peter Handke, *Falsche Bewegung* (Frankfurt am Main: 1975), p. 77.

5. Ibid., p. 81.

6. Wim Wenders to author (Los Angeles), 2 August 1980.

7. Hans Günther Pflaum, *Filmkorrespondenz,* no. 2 (1975), p. 11. For more on the connection between *Wrong Move* and the Bildungsroman, see Shelley Frisch, "The Disenchanted Image: From Goethe's *Wilhelm Meister* to Wenders' *Wrong Movement,*" *Literature/ Film Quarterly,* Summer 1979, pp. 208–14.

8. Hubert Niogret, "Entretien avec Wim Wenders," *Positif,* November 1976, p. 27.

9. Eberhard Seybold, "Die Regisseure sind richtige Gauner," *Frankfurter Neue Presse,* 18 June 1977.

10. Niogret, "Entretien," p. 28.

11. Fritz Müller-Scherz and Wim Wenders, *Kings of the Road,* photoscript trans. Christopher Doherty (Munich: 1976).

12. Jan Dawson, *Wim Wenders* (New York: 1976), p. 19.

13. "Rote Sonne," *Filmkritik,* January 1970, p. 9.

14. "Drei Rivalen," *Filmkritik,* October 1969, p. 618.

15. Heiko R. Blum, "Gespräch mit Wim Wenders," *Filmkritik,* February 1972, p. 74.

16. "Drei Rivalen," p. 618.

17. James Monaco, "Kings of the Road," *The Villager,* 14 October 1976.

18. Jörg Ulrich, "Handke denkt an Goethe," *Münchener Merkur,* 14 April 1975.

19. Wim Wenders to Ann Arbor Film Co-op, 6 April 1978.

20. Rentschler, *West German Film,* p. 178.

21. Michel Boujut, *Wim Wenders* (Paris: 1982), p. 8.

22. Carlos Clarens, "King of the Road," *Film Comment,* September–October 1977, p. 45.

23. "Die Männer dieser Generation," *Filmreport* 5–6, 1976.

24. Wim Wenders to author (Ann Arbor, Mich.), 7 April 1978.

25. Although he told a confidant that he would find it repulsive to shake a black man's hand, Hitler did not publicly snub Jesse Owens, a myth apparently started by the American press. While he was in Berlin, Owens, whose celebrity had preceded him, rivaled Hitler in popularity among the Germans. After narrowly defeating the German contender Lutz Long in the broad jump, Owens walked arm-in-arm with him around the track. It is unlikely that any young athelete of the time would have refused to shake his hand; most would have been thrilled to kiss his feet. (See Richard D. Mandell, *The Nazi Olympics* (Urbana, Ill.: 1987), pp. 167 and 226ff.) *Wrong Move*'s version of the Third Reich is therefore mythic just as Wilhelm's view of the adversarial role he must play vis à vis the older generation is mythic.

26. "Ich kann diese Jugend nicht leiden," *Twen,* May 1961, p. 48. Habe's wound metaphor recalls the emphasis on them in *Wrong Move;* Wilhelm's bloodied fist after he puts his hand through the window, Laertes' chronic nosebleed, and the industrialist's self-inflicted pencil wound. For more on this see Frisch, "Disenchanted Image," pp. 210ff.

27. Dawson, *Wenders,* p. 7.

28. According to Kreuzer, Wenders hadn't written her part yet when she arrived on location so she insisted on appearing with the candle. Lisa Kreuzer to author (Munich), 21 February 1980.

29. Tom Farrell, "Nick Ray's German Friend, Wim Wenders," *Wide Angle* 5:4 (1983), p. 62.

30. "Der Tod ist keine Lösung," *Der Spiegel,* 9 August 1976, p. 92.

31. Dawson, *Wenders,* p. 7.

Chapter 6

1. Filmverlag der Autoren, *"Der amerikanische Freund,"* promotion brochure.

2. Sven Hansen, "Mord aus Ratlosigkeit," *Die Welt* (Bonn), 5 August 1977.

3. Michael Covino, "Wim Wenders, a Worldwide Homesickness," *Film Quarterly,* Winter 1977–78, p. 15.

4. Martin Müller to author (Munich), 27 November 1979.

5. Filmverlag, *"Der amerikanische Freund."*

6. See Peter Handke, "Die privaten Weltkriege der Patricia Highsmith," *Der Spiegel,* 13 January 1975, p. 88.

7. Heiko R. Blum, "Gespräch mit Wim Wenders," *Filmkritik,* February 1972, p. 76.

8. Lisa Kreuzer to author, 21 February 1980.

9. Filmverlag, *"Der amerikanische Freund."*

10. Jan Dawson, "Filming Highsmith," *Sight and Sound,* Winter 1977–78, p. 36.

11. *The Politics of Cultural Despair* (Berkeley: 1961), p. 131.

12. Ibid., p. 132.

13. Claudia Sander von Dehn, "In der Endzeit des Kinos," *Hessische Allgemeine,* 9 July 1977.

14. Wim Wenders to author (Los Angeles), 2 August 1980.

15. Cf. for example, *F.I.S.T.*(Norman Jewison, 1977) where Sylvester Stallone returns to an unexpectedly empty house, searches it, and is gunned down by his enemies.

16. Alain Masson and Hubert Niogret, "Entretien avec Wim Wenders," *Positif,* October 1977, p. 21.

17. Jan Dawson, *Wim Wenders* (New York: 1976), p. 23.

18. "The Open Window and the Storm-Tossed Boat: An Essay in the Iconography of Romanticism," *Art Bulletin* 37:286.

19. Dawson, *Wim Wenders,* p. 23. Eric Rentschler and Peter Buchka have both noted the resemblance between Friedrich's "Wanderer Above the Mists" (1818) and the last shot in *Wrong Move* in which Wilhelm looks out from the Zugspitze over the German Alps. Although Rentschler finds the comparison ironic, for Wilhelm clearly does not possess the mastery over "the mists" that Friedrich's figure does, both figures share the romantic longing that Wenders and Eitner speak of. (See Eric Rentschler, *West German Film in the Course of Time* [Bedford Hills, N.Y.: 1984], p. 178 and Peter Buchka, *Augen kann man nicht kaufen: Wim Wenders und seine Filme* [Frankfurt am Main: 1985], pp. 70–71.)

Chapter 7

1. Terry Curtis Fox, "Wenders Crosses the Border," *Village Voice,* 30 October 1972.

2. Wim Wenders to Film Forum (New York), 21 May 1982.

3. Tim Hunter, "The Making of *Hammett,*" *New West,* 22 September 1980, p. 34.

4. Ibid., p. 36.

5. John Francis Kreidl, *Nicholas Ray* (Boston: 1977), p. 73.

6. Alain Masson and Hubert Niogret, "Entretien avec Wim Wenders," *Positif,* October, 1977, p. 24.

7. Hunter, "Making of *Hammett,*" p. 43.

8. Michel Ciment, "Entretien avec Wim Wenders," *Positif,* November 1982, p. 23.

9. Hunter, "Making of *Hammett,*" p. 43.

10. Jan Dawson, *Wim Wenders* (New York: 1976), p. 19.

11. Cf. Ferdinand's speech in Godard's *Pierrot le Fou:* "I've found an idea for a novel. No longer to write about people's lives . . . but only about life, life itself. What goes on between people, in space . . . like sound and colors."

12. "Movie Nuts (and Bolts)" *Village Voice,* 1 March 1983.

13. Chris Chase, "At the Movies," *New York Times,* 2 February 1983.

14. Michel Ciment, "Entretien avec Wim Wenders," *Positif,* November 1980, p. 16.

15. See chapter 5, n. 1.

16. Walter Adler, "Das grosse Geld, die Angst un der Traum von Geschichten Erzählen," *Filmkritik,* December 1978, p. 682.

17. Ciment, "Entretien" (1982), p. 21.

18. "Wim Wenders' *Hammett,*" *New York Times,* 1 July 1983.

19. "Ve Vere Young Then: The Filming of *Hammett,*" *Armchair Detective* 17:2 (1984), p. 123.

20. Ciment, "Entretien" (1982), p. 22.

21. See chapter 1, n. 17.

22. Chris Sievernich to author (New York), 16 June 1981.

23. "Transparencies on Film," trans. Thomas Y. Levin, *New German Critique*, Fall–Winter 1981–82, p. 206. (Orig. pub. in *Die Zeit*, 18 November 1966.)

24. Angelika Heinick, "Langsame Heimkehr," *Suddeutsche Zeitung*, 10–12 April 1982.

25. Dawson, *Wenders*, p. 17.

26. Donald Richie, *Ozu* (Berkeley: 1974), p. 10.

27. See chapter 3, n. 12.

Chapter 8

1. Don Ranvaud, *"Paris, Texas* to Sydney, Australia," *Sight and Sound*, Autumn 1984, p. 248.

2. *The Goalie's Anxiety at the Penalty Kick*, trans. Michael Roloff (New York: 1972), p. 11.

3. *Motel Chronicles* (San Francisco: 1982), pp. 22–24.

4. *Sam Shepard* (New York: 1985), p. 97; see also p. 129.

5. Michel Ciment and Hubert Niogret, "Entretien avec Wim Wenders," *Positif*, September 1984, p. 10.

6. Ibid.

7. Katherine Dieckmann, "Wim Wenders: An Interview," *Film Quarterly*, Winter 1984–85, p. 4.

8. *Motel Chronicles*, p. 104.

9. Ibid., p. 56.

10. *Hawk Moon Stories* (Los Angeles: 1973), p. 17.

11. Dieckmann, "Wim Wenders," p. 4.

12. Ibid., p. 3.

13. *Hawk Moon*, p. 50.

14. Ranvaud, *"Paris, Texas,"* p. 249.

15. Ibid.

16. Dieckmann, "Wim Wenders," p. 3.

17. See n. 5 above.

18. Dieckmann, "Wim Wenders," p. 5.

19. Ranvaud, *"Paris, Texas,"* p. 249.

20. Dieckmann, "Wim Wenders," pp. 5–7.

21. Ibid., p. 4.

22. Ranvaud, *"Paris, Texas,"* p. 249.

23. "Ist der Filmverlag noch zu retten?" *Süddeutsche Zietung*, 14 December 1984.

Appendix B

1. *Chronik der laufenden Ereignisse* (Frankfurt am Main: 1975), p. 130.

2. Horst Wiedemann, "Interview mit Robbie Müller," *Film und Ton Magazin,* May 1978, p. 69.

3. Filmverlag der Autoren, "Die linkshändige Frau," promotion brochure.

4. See Donald Ritchie, *Ozu* (Berkeley: 1974), pp. 136ff., cf. 174f. For more on the film's relationship to Ozu, see my "West Looks East: The Influence of Yasujiro Ozu on Wim Wenders and Peter Handke," *Art Journal,* Fall 1983, pp. 234–39.

5. For more on the film's literary aspects, see Timothy Corrigan, "The Tension of Translation: Handke's *The Left-Handed Woman* (1977)," in Eric Rentschler, *German Film and Literature: Adaptations and Transformations* (New York: 1986); further bibliography is appended to the Corrigan article.

Selected Bibliography

Books by Wenders

Wenders, Wim, and Fritz Müller-Scherz. *Kings of the Road*, photoscript. Translated by Christopher Doherty. Munich: 1976.

——, and Chris Sievernich. *Nick's Film: Lightning Over Water*, photoscript. Frankfurt am Main: 1981.

——, Sam Shepard and Chris Sievernich. *Paris, Texas*, photoscript. Nördlingen, West Germany: 1984.

——. *Texte zu Filmen und Musik*. Berlin: 1975. Collected articles originally appeared in *Film, Filmkritik, Süddeutsche Zeitung*, and *Twen* between 1968 and 1971.

——. *Tokyo-Ga*. English translation by David Vierling. Berlin: 1986.

——. *Wim Wenders' Emotion Pictures*. Frankfurt am Main: 1987.

Articles by Wenders

Wenders, Wim. "Der Tod ist keine Lösung." *Der Spiegel*, 9 August 1976. Reprinted in *Jahrbuch Film 77/78*, Munich 1977.

——. "Im Fernsehen: Furchtlose Flieger." *Filmkritik*, June 1971.

——. "Ins Kino vernarrt." *Berlinale-Tip*, January 1977. Reprinted in *Jahrbuch Film 77/78*, Munich: 1977.

——. "*Nashville*." *Die Zeit*, 21 May 1976.

——. "That's Entertainment: Hitler." *Die Zeit*, 12 August 1977.

——. "Wie eine kleine Abhängigkeit zur grossen wurde." *Süddeutsche Zeitung*, 14 December 1984.

Interviews with Wenders

Adler, Walter. "Das grosse Geld, die Angst und der Traum von Geschichten erzählen." *Filmkritik*, December 1978. (*Hammett*)

——. "Über die Produktion von *Hammett*." *Filmkritik*, February 1983.

Assayas, Olivier, and Serge Daney. "Entretien avec Wim Wenders." *Cahiers du cinéma*, December 1980.

Blum, Heiko R. "Gespräch mit Wim Wenders." *Filmkritik*, February 1972. (*Goalie*)

Bühler, Wolf Eckhart, and Paul B. Kleiser. "*Alice in den Städten*." *Filmkritik*, March 1974.

Chaillet, Jean-Paul. "*Hammett* n'est pas un film noir!" *Les Nouvelles litteraires*, 9 June 1982.

Ciment, Michel. "Entretien avec Wim Wenders." *Positif*. November 1980.

——. "Entretien avec Wim Wenders." *Positif*, November 1982.

Ciment, Michel and Hubert Niogret. "Entretien avec Wim Wenders." *Positif*, September 1984. (*Paris, Texas*)

Clarens, Carlos. "King of the Road." *Film Comment,* September–October 1977. (*American Friend*)
Dawson, Jan. "Filming Highsmith." *Sight and Sound,* Winter 1977–78.
——. *Wim Wenders.* New York: 1976.
Dieckmann, Katherine. "Wim Wenders: An Interview." *Film Quarterly,* Winter 1984–85. (*Paris, Texas*)
F. H. "Die Männer dieser Generation." *Filmreport* 5–6, 1976. (*Kings*)
Lachman, Edward, Peter Lehman, and Robin Wood. "Wim Wenders: An Interview." *Wide Angle,* 2:4 (1978).
Masson, Alain, and Hubert Niogret. "Entretien avec Wim Wenders." *Positif,* October 1977.
Müller-Scherz, Fritz, and Horst Wiedemann. "Wim Wenders über 'Im Lauf der Zeit.' " *Film und Ton Magazin,* May 1976.
Niogret, Hubert. "Entretien avec Wim Wenders." *Positif,* November 1976.
Pflaum, Hans Günther. *Filmkorrespondenz,* no. 2, 1975. (*Wrong Move*)
Rabourdin, Dominque. "Entretien avec Wim Wenders." *Cinéma 80,* December 1980. (*Lightning*)
Rayns, Tony. "Forms of Address: Interviews with Three German Filmmakers." *Sight and Sound,* Winter 1974–75.
Thompson, Bill. "A Young German Filmmaker and His Road Movie." *1000 Eyes,* November 1976.

Books about Wenders

Boujut, Michel. *Wim Wenders.* Paris: 1982.
Buchka, Peter. *Augen kann man nicht kaufen: Wim Wenders und seine Filme.* Frankfurt am Main: 1985.
Delvaux, Claudine, Philippe Dubois and Catherine Petit. *Les voyages de Wim Wenders.* Crisnée, Belgium: 1985.
Grob, Norbert. *Die Formen des filmischen Blicks: Wenders, die frühen Filme.* Munich: 1984.
Johnston, Shiela. *Wim Wenders.* London: 1981.
Künzel, Uwe. *Wim Wenders.* Freiburg: 1981.

Chapters Devoted to Wenders

Corrigan, Timothy. "Wenders's *Kings of the Road:* The Voyage from Desire to Language." In Corrigan, *New German Film: The Displaced Image.* Austin, Tex.: 1983.
Franklin, James. "Wim Wenders." In Franklin, *New German Cinema: From Oberhausen to Hamburg.* Boston: 1983.
Geist, Kathe. "Wenders in the Cities." In Klaus Phillips, *New German Filmmakers: From Oberhausen through the 1970s.* New York: 1984.
Harcourt, Peter. "Adaptation through Inversion: Wenders' *Wrong Movement.*" In Andrew Horton and Joan Magretta, *Modern European Filmmakers and the Art of Adaptation.* New York: 1981.
Rentschler, Eric. "Wim Wenders's Rerouting of Handke's *Wrong Move.*" In Rentschler, *West German Film in the Course of Time.* Bedford Hills, N.Y.: 1984.
Sandford, John. "Wim Wenders." In Sandford, *The New German Cinema.* London: 1980.

Articles on Wenders

Andrews, Nigel. "Wim Wenders/The Goalkeeper's Fear of the Penalty." *Sight and Sound,* Winter 1972–73.
Blum, Heiko R. "Die Verfemte von Salem." *Der Tagesspiegel* (Berlin), 11 March 1973.
Blumenberg, Hans C. "Deutschlands tote Seelen." *Die Zeit,* 21 March 1975. (*Wrong Move*)
——. "Ripley in den Städten." *Die Zeit,* 1 July 1977.
Buchka, Peter. ". . . in die leere Welt hinein." *Süddeutsche Zeitung,* 13–14 December 1975.
Canby, Vincent. "The Goalie's Anxiety." *New York Times,* 14 January 1977.
——. "The Last Months of Nicholas Ray's Life." *New York Times,* 26 September 1981.

——. *"Tokyo-Ga."* *New York Times,* 26 April 1985.

Corrigan, Timothy. "Cinematic Snuff: German Friends and Narrative Murders." *Cinema Journal,* Winter 1985.

——. "The Realist Gesture in the Films of Wim Wenders: Hollywood and the New German Cinema." *Quarterly Review of Film Studies,* Spring 1980.

Daney, Serge. "Wim's movie." *Cahiers du cinéma,* December 1980. (*Lightning*)

Donner, Wolf. "Open End." *Die Zeit,* 25 February 1972. (*Goalie*)

——. "Zwei Träumer unterwegs." *Die Zeit,* 5 March 1976. (*Kings*)

Ebert, Jürgen. "Der Tod ist ein grausames Märchen." *Filmkritik,* October 1981. (*Lightning*)

——. *"Im Lauf der Zeit I."* *Filmkritik,* July 1976.

Eder, Klaus. *"Alice in den Städten."* *Medium,* March 1974.

——. "Spiel-Sätze-Bilder." *Medium,* February 1972. (*Goalie*)

"Ein Kampf um *Paris, Texas."* *Der Spiegel.* 7 January 1985.

Farrell, Tom. "Nick Ray's German Friend, Wim Wenders." *Wide Angle,* 5:4 (1983).

Feldmann, Sebastien. *"Im Lauf der Zeit II."* *Filmkritik,* July 1976.

Fell, J. L. "The Wrong Movement." *Film Quarterly,* Winter 1978–79.

Feurich, J. P. *"Summer in the City."* *Filmkritik,* December 1971.

Fox, Terry Curtis. "Wenders Crosses the Border." *Village Voice,* 3 October 1977.

Frenais, Jacques. *"L'ami américain."* *Cinéma 77,* October 1977.

Frisch, Shelley. "The Disenchanted Image: From Goethe's *Wilhelm Meister* to Wenders' *Wrong Movement."* *Literature/Film Quarterly,* Summer 1979.

Garfield, Brian. "Ve Vere Young Then: The Filming of *Hammett,"* *Armchair Detective,* Spring 1984.

Geist, Kathe. "Filmmaking as Research: Wim Wenders' *The State of Things."* *Post Script,* Winter 1986.

——. *"Lightning Over Water."* *Film Quarterly,* Winter 1981.

——. "West Looks East: The Influence of Yasujiro Ozu on Wim Wenders and Peter Handke." *Art Journal,* Fall 1983.

Ghali, Nourredine. "Wim Wenders." *Cinéma 76,* December 1976.

Grafe, Frieda. "Erhebung überm Meeresspiegel." *Süddeutsche Zeitung,* 11 April 1975. (*Wrong Move*)

Grant, Jacques. *"Alice dans les villes."* *Cinéma 77,* July 1977.

——. *"Au fils du temps."* *Cinéma 76,* June 1976.

——. *"Faux movement."* *Cinéma 76,* January 1976.

Heinick, Angelika. "Langsame Heimkehr." *Süddeutsche Zeitung,* 10–12 April 1982.

Hoberman, John. *"Chambre 666* and *Reverse Angle."* *Village Voice,* 29 January 1985.

——. "Movie Nuts and Bolts." *Village Voice,* 1 March 1983. (*State of Things*)

Honickel, Thomas. "Wim im Land der unbegrenzten Möglichkeiten: Über die Geschichte der 'Hammett' Verfilmung." *Film und Ton Magazin,* June 1981.

Hunter, Tim. "The Making of *Hammett."* *New West,* 22 September 1980.

Jenny, Urs. "Männer unterwegs." *Der Spiegel,* January 1985. (*Paris, Texas*)

Jeremias, Brigitte. "Die hoffnungslose Jugend der 70er Jahren." *Frankfurter Allgemeine Zeitung,* 20 March 1975. (*Wrong Move*)

Kaufman, Stanley. "Wenders." *New Republic,* 29 January 1977.

Keenan, Richard C., and James M. Welsh. "Wim Wenders and Nathaniel Hawthorne: From *The Scarlet Letter* to *Der scharlachrote Buchstabe."* *Literature/Film Quarterly,* Spring 1978.

Keogh, Peter. "The Japanese Friend." *Chicago Reader,* 7 June 1985. (*Tokyo-Ga*)

Kinder, Marsha. *"The American Friend."* *Film Quarterly,* Winter 1978–79.

Le Pavec, Jean-Pierre. "Nick's movie, un cinéma au carré." *Cinéma 80,* December 1980.

Magny, Joël. "Wim Wenders entre classicisme et modernité." *Cinéma 84,* September 1984.

Masson, Alain. "Le romanesque et la spectaculaire." *Positif,* October 1977. (*American Friend*)

Meerapfel, Jeanine. "Komm, Keule, wir drehn ein heisses Bild." *Die Zeit Magazin,* 1 July 1977. (*American Friend*)

Monaco, James. "*Kings of the Road.*" *Villager,* 14 October 1976.
——. "Wim Wenders' *Alice in the Cities.*" *Take One,* May–June 1974.
Muthmann, W. F. "*Der scharlachrote Buchstabe.*" *Süddeutsche Zeitung,* 19 March 1973.
Pflaum, Hans Günther. "Ein sinnlicher, ein vitaler, ein makelloser Film." *Süddeutsche Zeitung,* 20 March 1976. (*Kings*)
Ranvaud, Don. "*Paris, Texas* to Sydney, Australia," *Sight and Sound,* Autumn 1984.
Rentschler, Eric. "How American Is it: The U.S. as Image and Imaginary in German Film." *Persistance of Vision,* Fall 1985.
Riehl-Heyse, Herbert. "Das Jahr mit dem amerikanischen Freund." *Süddeutsche Zeitung,* 19 March 1973.
Schlunk, Jürgen E. "The Image of America in German Literature and in the New German Cinema: *The American Friend.*" *Literature/Film Quarterly,* Summer 1979.
Schober, Siegfried. "Die Leiden des Wilhelm M." *Der Spiegel,* 10 March 1975.
——. "Mann und Kind." *Der Spiegel,* 4 March 1974. (*Alice*)
Schütte, Wolfram. " 'Es muss alles anders werden' oder Reisen von innen nach aussen." *Frankfurter Rundschau,* 30 March 1976. (*Kings*)
Steinhart, Peter. "Flippern, warten, weiterfliehen." *Rheinische Post,* 25 April 1972. (*Summer in the City*)
Sterritt, David. "German Director in U.S. Tradition." *Christian Science Monitor,* 15 January 1977.
Tarratt, Margaret. "*Kings of the Road.*" *Films and Filming,* May 1977.
Theuring, Gerhard. "Filme von Wim Wenders." *Filmkritik,* May 1969. (Short films)
Thome, Rudolf. "Es muss alles anders werden." *Berliner Wochenmagazin,* 12 March 1976. (*Kings*)
Van Gelder, Lawrence. "*Alice in the Cities.*" *New York Times,* 9 October 1974.
Welsh, Henry. "Cinéma et vidéo dans 'Nick's Movie.' " *Jeune Cinéma,* April–May 1981.
Wiedemann, Horst. "Das Freiheitsversprechen und die Frustration." *Film und Ton Magazin,* May 1976. (*Kings*)
Wiegand, Wilfried. "Kunstfigur aus Fleisch und Blut." *Frankfurter Allgemeine Zeitung,* 2 March 1972. (Short films)

Actors, Team, Filmverlag

Dietrichs, Helmut H. "Fangschuss für furchtlose Flieger." *Medium.* March 1977. (History of Filmverlag)
Goldschmidt, Didier. "Entretien avec Rudiger Volger." *Cinématographe.* February 1981.
Grant, Jacques. "Entretien avec Rudiger Vogler." *Cinéma 76,* December 1976.
Honickel, Thomas. "Schneiden ist ein Job wie jeder andere auch." *Film und Ton Magazin,* August 1979. (Interview with Peter Przygodda)
Jurczyk, Günter, "Changes in Producer Company Heralds End of an Era." *German Tribune,* 10 May 1987. Reprinted from the *Hannoversche Allgemeine,* 22 April 1987. (Filmverlag)
Lahann, Birgit. "Interview mit Lisa Kreuzer." *Brigitte,* no. 21 (1977).
Lehman, Peter. "Making Deals and Matching Actions: An Interview with Edward Lachman." *Wide Angle* 5:4 (1983).
Lubowski, Bernd. " 'Falsche Bewegung' und richtige Töne." *Berliner Morgenpost,* 26 June 1975. (Jürgen Knieper)
Scharres, Barbara. "Robby Müller and *Paris, Texas.*" *American Cinematographer,* February 1985.
Wiedemann, Horst. "Interview mit Robby Müller." *Film und Ton Magazin,* May 1978.
——. "Stil ist der Tod der Kamera." *Film und Ton Magazin,* April 1978. (Interview with Robby Müller)

Index